IMAGES OF

SALERNO To THE GUSTAV LINE 1943-1944

RARE PHOTOGRAPHS FROM WARTIME ARCHIVES

Jon Diamond

Pen & Sword
MILITARY

First published in Great Britain in 2018 by
PEN & SWORD MILITARY
An imprint of
Pen & Sword Books Ltd
47 Church Street
Barnsley
South Yorkshire
S70 2AS

ISBN 978-1-52670-734-5

Typeset by Concept, Huddersfield, West Yorkshire HD4 5JL.
Printed and bound by CPI Group (UK) Ltd, Croydon, CR0 4YY

Pen & Sword Books Limited incorporates the imprints of Atlas, Archaeology, Aviation, Discovery, Family History, Fiction, History, Maritime, Military, Military Classics, Politics, Select, Transport, True Crime, Air World, Frontline Publishing, Leo Cooper, Remember When, Seaforth Publishing, The Praetorian Press, Wharncliffe Local History, Wharncliffe Transport, Wharncliffe True Crime and White Owl.

For a complete list of Pen & Sword titles please contact
PEN & SWORD BOOKS LIMITED
47 Church Street, Barnsley, South Yorkshire S70 2AS, England
E-mail: enquiries@pen-and-sword.co.uk
Website: www.pen-and-sword.co.uk

Contents

Acknowledgements

This archival photograph volume in the *Images of War* series is dedicated to the men and women who fought and perished in southern and central Italy during the early autumn of 1943, and extending well into 1944, in order to wrest control of the Italian mainland from the Nazis. Upon viewing the photographs, we ponder the heroic sacrifice made to maintain freedom lest we forget. The author also wishes to acknowledge the many military history scholars, past and present, including such names as Blumenson, D'Este, Ellis, Neillands, Strawson, Konstam, Mason, Atkinson and Whitlock, who have catalogued the nuances of this harsh and protracted campaign with their superlative prose. The author is indebted to the able assistance of the archivists at both the United States Army Military History Institute (USAMHI) at the United States Army War College in Carlisle, Pennsylvania, and the Still Photo Section of the National Archives and Records Administration (NARA) in College Park, Maryland.

Chapter One

Strategic Prelude to the Invasion

The see-saw struggle across the North African littoral in the Mediterranean Theatre of Operations (MTO) ended with the British Eighth Army's victory over German and Italian forces at El Alamein in early November 1942. British prime minister Winston Churchill stated after the victory over Rommel's *Panzerarmee Afrika*: 'Now this is not the end; it is not even the beginning of the end. But it is, perhaps, the end of the beginning.' In his monumental post-war history Churchill wrote: 'Before Alamein we never had a victory. After Alamein, we never had a defeat.'

Concurrent with the final pursuit of the Axis forces throughout Libya, the Allies amphibiously invaded Vichy French-controlled Morocco and Algeria during Operation Torch on 8 November 1942. A brutal six-month campaign to drive the Axis from their 'Tunisgrad' bridgehead, and Africa entirely, ensued. The Allies victoriously entered Tunis on 8 May 1943 to a massive surrender of German and Italian forces.

To implement the large Allied force in North Africa and to secure the Mediterranean Sea lanes, Sicily was amphibiously assaulted by the US Seventh and British Eighth armies on 10 July 1943, Operation Husky. After a tenacious thirty-eight-day campaign, the Axis evacuated the island to the Italian mainland across the Strait of Messina. Mussolini was deposed on 24 July and representatives of the Italian government were secretly negotiating terms of an armistice with the Allies, which they signed on 3 September. A springboard for the invasion of Continental Europe via its soft underbelly was now in Allied hands. In the meantime, Hitler had been in the process of planning to seize control of Italy with *Wehrmacht* troops, if the Italians surrendered. The Italian capitulation was officially announced on 8 September.

Despite US Army planners not wanting to detract from their build-up of the nascent forces in Britain for a cross-Channel assault, the American joint chiefs of staff acquiesced to other Mediterranean amphibious operations: an invasion of the Italian mainland across the Strait of Messina by British XIII Corps along the Calabrian toe of Italy (Operation Baytown, 3 September); along the beaches of the Gulf of Salerno (Operation Avalanche, 9 September) by the Allied Fifth Army; and at the port of Taranto (Operation Slapstick, 9 September) by elements of the British 1st Airborne Division at the heel of the Italian Peninsula.

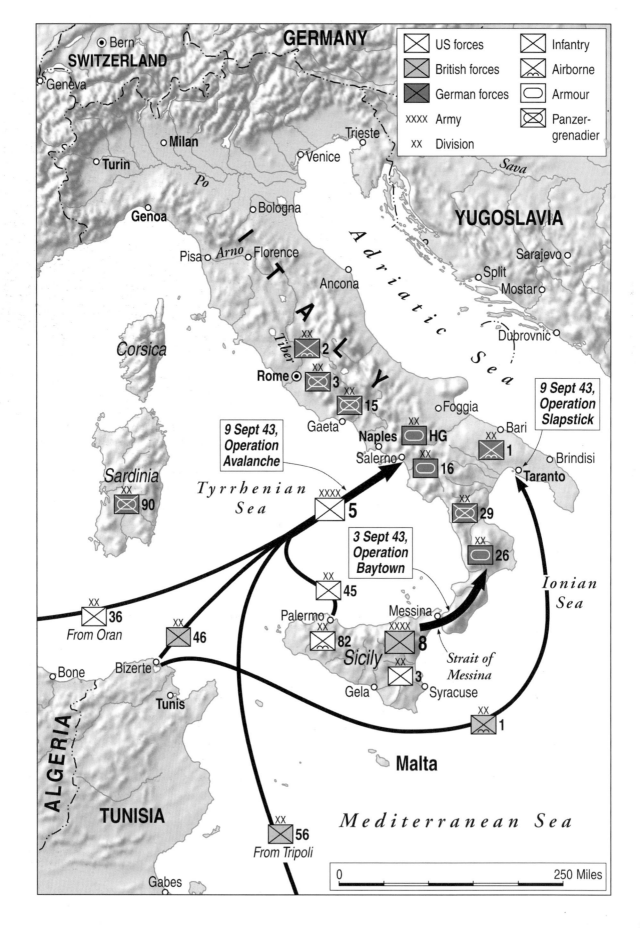

During the Second Battle of El Alamein in early November 1942, some of Lieutenant-General Bernard L. Montgomery's Eighth Army troops are shown taking cover from Axis artillery shell-bursts at the side of a disabled Panzer Mk IV. The Eighth Army's victory against German Field Marshal Erwin Rommel's *Panzerarmee Afrika* ended the see-saw two-year battle across the Cyrenaican and Egyptian deserts. Afterwards, the Axis forces began their lengthy westward retreat into Tunisia or surrendered. (*NARA*)

The Mediterranean Theatre of Operations, September 1943. Tunis and Bizerte fell to the Allies on 8 May 1943. Sicily was chosen as the next Allied MTO target as Operation Husky was launched on 10 July 1943. After thirty-eight days, the US Seventh and British Eighth armies conquered the island and the surviving Axis forces fled across the Strait of Messina to the Italian mainland. On 3 September 1943, during Operation Baytown, the British Eighth Army's XIII Corps invaded the Italian mainland at Reggio and other locales in Calabria. Six days later, Operation Slapstick, an uncontested amphibious assault on the port of Taranto, was launched by elements of the British 1st Airborne Division. Also, on 9 September 1943, Operation Avalanche unfolded along the beaches in the Gulf of Salerno to secure a foothold for the Allied Fifth Army to be in proximity to the port-city of Naples. Allied forces sailed from several MTO ports including: the US 36th Division from Oran; the British 46th and 1st Airborne divisions from Bizerte; the British 56th Division from Tripoli; and the US 45th Division from Palermo. The US 82nd Airborne and 3rd Infantry divisions waited in reserve on Sicily. General von Vietinghoff's German Tenth Army, with its 16th, 26th, and Hermann Göring Panzer divisions, the 3rd, 15th, and 29th Panzer Grenadier divisions was to launch massive counter-attacks. The positions of the 1st and 2nd *Luftwaffe* Parachute divisions in Italy as well as the 90th Panzer Grenadier Division on Sardinia are also shown. (*Philip Schwartzberg, Meridian Mapping, Minneapolis, MN*).

(**Above**) US soldiers from the Allied Western Task Force, under Lieutenant-General George S. Patton, are shown riding the carriage of a Bofors anti-aircraft (AA) gun onto the Atlantic shores of French Morocco near Safi on Operation Torch's D-Day, 8 November 1942. The Anglo-American invasion of Vichy French north-west Africa along the French Moroccan coast to seize Casablanca as well as in the Mediterranean at Oran and Algiers was intended to launch a quick strike for Tunis to permanently drive the Axis from North Africa. The German response to both the Allied invasion and Vichy capitulation was swift, commencing a bitter six-month campaign in Tunisia. (*NARA*)

(**Opposite, above**) An American reconnaissance Jeep is shown with its surviving crew from the three days of fighting at Sidi bou Zid, Tunisia, in mid-February 1943. On 14 February, tank columns from the German 5th *Panzer-armee*'s 21st and 10th Panzer divisions, under General Hans-Jürgen von Arnim's command, broke through a thin American armoured defensive line there. A failed American armoured and mechanised infantry counter-attack by major elements of the US 1st Armoured Division was crushed, leading to the capture of approximately 1,500 American soldiers, 150 American tanks and scores of half-tracks, artillery pieces and trucks, that left doubts among British commanders about the American forces' battle readiness against the veteran Nazis. (*NARA*)

(**Opposite, below**) A German 10th Panzer Division's Mk IV Panzer is shown lying disabled on the Tunisian desert valley floor near El Guettar, where American II Corps forces now under Lieutenant-General George S. Patton's command defeated this Nazi formation on 23 March 1943. The 1st Infantry Division's 16th and 18th Infantry Regiments repelled two German Panzers and motorised infantry assaults, with *Luftwaffe* cover, utilising massed artillery, tank destroyers, mines, air sorties and hand-to-hand combat. This combat provided a diversion of Nazi armour away from the British Eighth Army in the south. Also, American and British commanders were pleased with how much the US II Corps' fighting *élan* had improved since the battlefield disasters at Sidi bou Zid and Kasserine. (*NARA*)

(**Above**) The crew of a British Eighth Army Universal carrier is shown reading a sign in French in the Tunisian town of Mareth after its capture in late March 1943. The term Universal applied to the carrier was apt since it could be used for a variety of combat functions from simply moving infantry or being armed with a Bren light or Vickers medium machine-gun, an antiquated Boys anti-tank rifle, or a mortar. The Mareth Line consisted of a series of outdated blockhouses and entrenchments built by the French in the late 1930s to protect southern Tunisia from Mussolini's Tripolitania outposts. Rommel had doubts of the suitability of the Mareth Line to stop Montgomery's Eighth Army and left Africa permanently on 9 March with Arnim assuming command of *Panzerarmeegruppe Afrika*. (*NARA*)

(**Opposite, above**) US soldiers from the 60th Infantry Regiment of the 9th Division are shown marching in single-file holding their M1 semi-automatic Garand rifles along one of the hills surrounding a valley 7 miles outside the Tunisian port of Bizerte on 7 May 1943. That day marked the fall of the port after vicious house-to-house fighting in the city that utilised M3 Medium Lee tanks and 9th Division infantry. Bizerte had been assigned to US II Corps for capture and had once been part of the Nazi bridgehead for supply and reinforcement after Operation Torch commenced six months earlier. (*USAMHI*)

(**Opposite, below**) Infantrymen of the Princess Patricia Canadian Light Infantry (PPCLI) are seen leaving a grove of fruit trees to make their way through barbed wire to cross an open field on Sicily in July 1943. Encountering only cursory opposition from ill-equipped and poorly trained Italian coastal defenders, 1st Canadian Division made their combat debut exit from their beachhead to advance north-westerly prior to beginning a British XXX Corps' arc around the Monte Etna massif, Operation Hardgate. (*NARA*)

(**Opposite, above**) Elements of the US 2nd Armoured Division, under Major-General Hugh Gaffey, are shown moving down a Palermo street on 22 July 1943 to the cheers of some of the Sicilian capital's residents. The entire island's capture on 17 August enabled the Allied invasion of the Italian mainland, despite protests from some American planners fearing a distraction from the Allied build-up in the United Kingdom for a future cross-Channel invasion of Normandy. (*NARA*)

(**Opposite, below**) A British infantry section is seen advancing through the rubble of heavily defended Catania, which was subjected to intense Allied aerial bombing, artillery shelling and naval gunfire. British XIII Corps took Augusta on 12 July 1943. However, Catania did not fall until 5 August, due to an inability to properly deploy British formations along the narrow axis of advance in the vicinity of the heavily defended Monte Etna massif. (*NARA*)

(**Above**) Forward elements of the US 3rd Infantry Division enter the north-eastern Sicilian port of Messina after the Axis had executed an evacuation from the island across the Strait of Messina during Operation Lehrgang. During the exodus across the Strait, approximately 62,000 Italian and 40,000 Germans arrived in Calabria. About fifty Nazi tanks, along with 10,000 vehicles and approximately 200 artillery pieces, were ferried across the waterway for future operations against the Allies wherever they were to mount an amphibious assault on the Italian mainland. (*NARA*)

After Messina's capture, Lieutenant-General Bernard L. Montgomery (*left*), British Eighth Army commanding general and General Dwight D. Eisenhower (*right*), Allied Forces Commander, Mediterranean Theatre of Operations (MTO) are shown scanning the Strait of Messina from the Sicilian harbour toward their next objective, Reggio di Calabria on the Italian mainland. On 3 September, Operation Baytown would commence with Operations Slapstick and Avalanche to begin on 9 September. (*NARA*)

Chapter Two

Terrain, Fortifications and Weapons

Allied planners concluded that the Gulf of Naples beaches were an unsuitable locale for amphibious assault to secure the Neapolitan port-city. Allied naval commanders feared fortified sea defences and the heights of Monte Vesuvius dominating the coast. As alternative landing areas, the Fifth Army could land either 25 miles north-west of the city near the mouth of the Volturno River in the Gulf of Gaeta, or 50 miles south-east of Naples along the beaches of the Gulf of Salerno.

A landing in the Volturno River area in the Gulf of Gaeta was considered, as the disembarking Allied assault troops would be able to exit from the landing beaches and get onto the open Naples Plain, a terrain ideal for tanks and in proximity for an armoured thrust into the outskirts of the city. A Gulf of Gaeta assault was intended to deny the Nazi defenders the surrounding hills or other terrain features that would impede a rapid deployment from the beachhead into the environs of Naples. However, this invasion site was too remote for the Allied fighter bases on Sicily to provide an air umbrella for an amphibious assault. Also, invading near the mouth of the Volturno River was too far north from the British Eighth Army's Calabrian landing sites for mutual support of the Allied Fifth Army in a timely manner. Other naval disadvantages for a Gulf of Gaeta amphibious assault included the mined and fortified maritime approaches and an unfavourable hydrographic gradient of an offshore sandbar that precluded Allied transports from landing close to shore.

The Gulf of Salerno, with its 25-mile stretch of beaches south of the town of Salerno to Agropoli, offered the most favourable conditions for a landing that was within reach of Allied air cover. The beaches had little surf and an offshore gradient permitted transports to come to the shoreline. Allied planners envisioned easy construction of beach exits from the narrow strip separating the water and dunes. The terrain behind the dunes was suitable for supply dumps. The small port of Salerno and the nearby harbour of Amalfi were assets for unloading supplies. The coastal road was expected to enhance transportation of troops and supplies. Enemy fortifications at Salerno were mostly of the fieldwork type rather than permanent concrete fortifications.

However, there were terrain features at Salerno that heightened the Allied amphibious invasion's risks. The narrow 10-mile-wide crescent-shaped coastal plain was ringed by rugged mountains. The Sorrento Peninsula, at the southern end of the Gulf of Naples with the town of Salerno at its eastern base, was the north-west portion of the mountain wall that arced inland and southward until it met the sea again at Agropoli.

Two principal rivers ran through Salerno's coastal plain – the Sele and Calore, the latter being a tributary of the former. Both waterways ran parallel for 7 miles and were fordable at several points before their junction 4 miles from the coast, with the Sele emptying into the Gulf of Salerno about 17 miles south of the town of Salerno. The Sele River divided the coastal plain into two distinct sectors that became isolated battlefields – a northern half, where British X Corps landed, and a southern one that was assaulted by the US VI Corps. The dividing nature of the Sele River's geography compelled the Allies to bring bridging equipment onto the assault beaches to span the river for communication between the Fifth Army's two corps.

Monte Eboli stretched 8 miles north of the Sele River with the town of Eboli located on the lower eastern slopes. South-east of Eboli and Sele and Calore rivers, the town of Altavilla was situated halfway up Hill 424 at the northern end of a chain of heights. At its southern end, the hill chain joined Monte Soprano, with sheer cliffs 3,000 feet above sea level that dominated the beaches at Paestum, where US VI Corps landed. Montes Eboli and Soprano viewed from a distance rose from the coastal plain and towered high above the foothills.

The Sorrento Peninsula's rocky spur ascended from the shoreline and limited the depth of the initial beachhead at Salerno by isolating the major roadways to the interior from the landing areas via two narrow gorges that traversed the mountain mass, the Chiunzi and Molina passes. If Allied troops did not secure these mountain passes during the initial assault, the enemy had the terrain and tactical advantages to delay the drive on Naples as well as expose the assault forces to enemy observation, artillery fire and counter-attack from the surrounding heights. Narrow valleys also restricted armoured forces and limited their movement to the coastal plain.

Two of the major north-south roads of lower Italy crossed Salerno's coastal plain. Highway 18, the coastal road, was the chief German route of approach from the north. Highway 19 ran up the coastal plain from the south, intersecting Highway 18 at Battipaglia. Two railway lines followed almost the same paths as the roads. The only settlement on the Salerno plain was at Paestum, near an ancient Greek temple. Battipaglia, Eboli, Albanella, Capaccio and other villages that were to figure prominently were either at the very foot of the mountains or situated on their slopes. Below the hills, which were covered with olive orchards and orange groves, stretched well-cultivated fields on the coastal plain. The Allied forces were to fight their way from the beaches across the level plain, over the foothills to the mountain passes, and through the passes to Naples. Another feature of the Salerno battlefield was the airfield complex at Montecorvino, in proximity to the assault shoreline, at which the Allied planners wanted to station four fighter squadrons.

In addition to the Sele and Calore rivers at the Salerno beachhead, a number of other rivers were to be prominent in the Italian Campaign throughout the remainder of 1943 and extending into the winter months of 1944. The Volturno rose in the mountains near Isernia and descended to the vicinity of Venafro. Then it turned south-east and paralleled the coast about 30 miles inland for a distance of about 25 miles. Near the village of Amorosi, after being joined by the waters of the Calore River, it twisted south-west through an intensely cultivated farm valley flanked by scrub-covered hills and barren mountains to the Triflisco Gap. From there, at the beginning of the coastal belt, the Volturno meandered in large tight loops through olive groves to the sea at Castel Volturno. The Volturno was a formidable obstacle and, although fordable at most points (depth of 3 to 5 feet), the river was in flood stage as the Allies approached. The swift current mandated the initial the use of boats to cross its 150 to 200-foot width. The river's slick and steep 5 to 15-foot banks were to hamper landings, too.

British X Corps was to assault the Volturno's coastal region, which comprised level area of fertile farmland, vineyards and olive groves. US VI Corps was to cross to the east in an uplands area of rocky peaks, deep gorges and overhanging cliffs. Brush and olive groves on the far shore provided enemy concealment, whereas open fields on the near side gave no covered approaches to the crossing sites. German General von Vietinghoff placed the 35,000 men of the XIV Panzer Corps behind the Volturno's northern bank. The Allied Fifth Army drive across the Volturno River on the night of 12–13 October 1943 was to be complicated by autumn rains, flooded streams and enemy demolished roads and bridges.

Leaving the Volturno River Plain, Highway Number 6, which coursed through the Liri Valley and then onto Rome, followed a natural corridor through the north-to-south Apennine Mountains barrier, which was more than 6,000 feet high and snow-capped. This formidable mountain chain was a force multiplier for the Germans as it separated the two Allied armies from mutual support. However, the Germans did move units across the chain along interior lines. The Mignano Gap, 600 to 700 feet above sea level, was a vital mile-wide corridor through the mountains. The gap's southern pillar was Monte Camino, about 3,000 feet in height, with even more prominent ridges to the north, including Montes la Difensa and Maggiore. Just beyond the Mignano Gap, as the valley began to widen out again toward the Rapido River plain, two small, roughly 600-foot hills were situated across the corridor: Montes Rotondo and Lungo, which blocked the exits from the mountains. Just to the north of Highway 6 was the town of San Pietro, with Monte Sammucro to its north.

The swiftly flowing Rapido River, 25–50 feet wide with steep banks, coursed tortuously from its mountainous origin north of Monte Cassino and weaved in a southerly direction in front of Cassino, which was to become one of the most fortified towns during the Italian Campaign. The Germans had diverted the river upstream from the assault area, making the approaches a sea of mud. The high ground on the far bank of the Rapido River, of which Monte Cassino formed a part, comprised a series of heights. From the heights of Monte Cassino and Sant' Angelo, the Germans observed and brought fire on the entire area below. Some 2 miles to the west, Monte Cairo overlooked the lower heights from its peak over 5,000 feet high, with the remaining heights ranging between 1,500 and 3,000 feet. As a final hurdle, troops who attempted to debouch into the Rapido Valley found themselves facing two isolated hills, Montes Trocchio and Porchia at 1,400 and 800 feet, respectively. Both of these isolated hills were directly on the approach to Cassino and flanked the plain leading across the Rapido River into the Liri Valley. The 36th Division's late January 1944 attack across the Rapido River was doomed to fail as long as Monte Cassino, along with the hill country to the north and west, was possessed by the Nazis. In these mountainous defensive positions, the Germans positioned artillery and mortar regiments to rain fire on the entire offensive area of the 36th Division and large parts of the rear area of US II Corps.

Several miles downstream, the Rapido flowed into the Liri River near Sant' Ambroglio and then the confluence of both waterways became the Garigliano River, which then flowed south-west for 15 miles to the sea. The Rapido-Garigliano floodplain and the steep uplands beyond it constituted the western end of the *Gustav* Line (see below). Another 5-mile-wide floodplain was also situated near the Garigliano River's mouth on the eastern side of the waterway, which made an attack across this area very hazardous.

The Liri Valley gave the Germans all the natural defensive advantages. To the south the valley was flanked by steep mountains, which bordered the western side of the Garigliano all the way from the sea to the river's bend into the Liri Valley. To the east the mountain range widened north from Monte Sammucro to the Apennines, protecting the approach to the Liri Valley from the north via the Rapido Valley. This range was dominated by peaks nearing 4,000 feet, was poorly inhabited, and almost devoid of natural routes of communication for the advance of an army. Only two tortuous and narrow roads traversed this desolate landscape dominated by hilly peaks. The first one ran to Sant' Elia Flumerapido, north of Cassino, while the second coursed from where the Rapido made a north-eastward bend to a mountainous area between Colle Belvedere and Monte Cifalco and then north-westward to Atina.

The Sangro River on Italy's Adriatic coast was an excellent barrier as heavy rains in the nearby snow-capped mountains caused flooding, which limited the ability for fording. Situated behind a low-lying plain, the main German defense system was established on a ridge based on two strongly fortified villages, Mozzogrogna and Fossacesia. Montgomery's Eighth Army was to mount an attack up the Adriatic coast towards Ortona. On capturing this Adriatic port, the Eighth Army was to advance on Pescara and then swing west on Highway 5 towards Rome and outflank the rear of the German forces there in the Rome Line. On the night of 19–20 November, the Eighth Army attacked through the Winter Line (see below) on the lower Sangro River, and it was immediately engaged in heavy fighting with the Germans contesting the entire frontage in the hills overlooking the river.

The Winter Line, built by the Todt Organisation utilising enemy reserve troops and forced civilian labour, referred to a series of well-prepared German fortifications along the waist of Italy from the Garigliano River in the west through the mountains in the centre to the Sangro River in the east. The Winter Line was comprised of three belts of German fortifications, each with a succession of interlocked defences in depth. No single key position presented an opportunity for an Allied *coup de main* that could break the entire system. A mountain massif and nearby valley in the Winter Line had to be captured before the next mountainous defence position was assaulted. It was Kesselring's intent that the Allies would 'break their teeth' trying to pierce these defences.

The Winter Line's primary belt was the Gustav Line, which ran across Italy from just north of where the Garigliano River flows into the Tyrrhenian Sea. Monte Cassino and the Garigliano and Rapido rivers were the terrain anchors of this inter-locking zone of fortified bunkers and artillery positions. The Gustav Line extended east through the Apennine Mountains to the mouth of the Sangro River on the Adriatic coast.

There were also two subsidiary fortification belts, the Bernhardt and the Hitler lines, both of which ran much shorter distances from the Tyrrhenian Sea to just north-east of Cassino, where they would merge into the Gustav Line. These two fortification lines depended primarily on hastily erected defences composed of barbed concertina wire 50–75 feet in depth, log and earth bunkers, and mutually supporting automatic weapon pits. Concrete and steel pillboxes were encountered as the Allies approached the Gustav Line. The Bernhardt Line ran through Mignano, 50 miles to the north of Naples, and extended from a bend in the Garigliano River inland from the coast, near San Ambrogio. The Bernhardt Line then ran through the range of Montes Camino, Maggiore and Sammucro to extend northwards to Castel di Sangro in the middle of the peninsula. The Germans had laid 45,000 mines in the Bernhardt Line and another 30,000 on its approaches. Relative to the Gustav Line, the minor Hitler Line stood 10 miles to the south-east.

The most forward line of Nazi fortifications was a hastily prepared series of out-posts called the Barbara Line. This ill-defined group of defensive works ran from Mondragone near the Tyrrhenian coast through the villages of Teano and Presenzano and then into the Matese Mountains, to the south-east of Venafro and Isernia. German General von Vietinghoff was ordered to hold out along the Volturno River line until at least 15 October in order that the more permanent fortifications of the Winter Line could be completed.

Along the entire frontage of Clark's Fifth Army, the Germans were expert at erecting fortifications and using terrain to delay the Allied movement. Mutually supporting automatic weapon-and-mortar pits were buried deep within rock formations to cover all Allied advance routes. German minefields were sown on roads, trails, gullies, and in valleys between the mountains. Bridges and culverts were destroyed to hamper Allied vehicle and armour movement. River crossings were to be delayed by extensive mining of riverbanks, in addition to diverting waterways to create flood areas. With some rivers at flood stage or above, the Allies would have to use assault boats as high water prevented the timely installation of assault bridges.

When the Allies had to combat Nazi troops in Italian towns and villages, stone-built homes were transformed into small forts requiring both indirect artillery and direct small field guns and tanks to reduce the positions. Street fighting became a necessity against a tenacious enemy using rocky rubble as breastworks. Booby traps and mines were also sown in these village strongpoints to delay the Allied advance.

During the mountain warfare in southern Italy, control of the heights above determined which combatant dominated the valley below. The Nazi defensive positions atop mountain peaks became force multipliers. Exploiting the rugged terrain, the Germans used a small number of well-chosen strongpoints to slow the numerically superior Allied forces almost to a standstill from the Salerno beachhead. German Howitzers and long-range guns, some self-propelled and others well-defiladed behind protecting crests, reached nearly every Allied area and placed them under near-constant harassing shellfire. Mountain peaks provided posts from which German forward observers noted every Allied movement during daylight hours. Thus, much of the Fifth Army's advances had to be made under the cover of darkness or smoke. Interior lines benefitted the Nazi defenders as they re-supplied and reinforced their frontline positions with relative ease and speed. German Field Marshal Kesselring proved to be a master at moving his forces deftly from one threatened position to another to repeatedly staunch an Allied thrust.

In addition to an orderly withdrawal after relinquishing defensive positions, German bridge destruction forced the advancing Allies to ford a series of rivers and streams under harassing enemy fire. Allied engineers had to erect temporary bridges in order to quickly reinforce the bridgeheads on the far banks once seized. Allied engineer units implemented bulldozers and Bailey bridges to propel the Allied advance across waterways, while sure-footed packed mules became the primary re-supply 'vehicle' in the mountainous terrain.

Monte Vesuvius, situated 6 miles to the east of Naples. In 79 AD, an eruption from the volcano destroyed the Roman city of Pompei. Above, it is shown erupting with ash as the Allies reached Naples in October 1943. In March 1944, the volcano fully erupted with lava pouring down its slopes. Neapolitan boats burned in the port while showers of molten rock and pumice ruined eighty B-25 bombers of the 340th Bombardment Group stationed at Pompei Airfield near Terzigno. Unlike Monte Etna's impact on British Eighth Army's movements on Sicily's eastern side, Monte Vesuvius was to have little strategic or tactical import on the Italian Campaign. *(NARA)*

(**Above**) Soldiers of the 36th Infantry Division are shown marching past the remains of the Greek Temple of Neptune at Paestum to the south-east of Salerno after landing on 9 September 1943. This ancient site was defended by German 16th Panzer Division machine-gunners and snipers on that D-Day. Later it became headquarters for the US 40th Port Battalion, charged with offloading supplies for the 36th Division. The Temple of Neptune was also situated in proximity to Clark's Fifth Army headquarters at the Bellelli Palace about a mile south-west of the junction of the Sele and Calore rivers. (*NARA*)

(**Opposite, above**) The Cassino battlefield is seen from Monte Trocchio to the south-east of the town of Cassino. The snow-capped 5,000-ft Monte Cairo is shown looming above the town with a castle on the hill (*right foreground*). The Benedictine abbey, in the left of the photograph, was situated high above both the town and Castle Hill. To the rear of the monastery's mount (*left background*), was the Liri Valley with Highway 6, which led to Rome. The Rapido River ran in a north-to-south direction, just to the east of Cassino town. (*NARA*)

(**Opposite, below**) US Fifth Army artillery spotters are perched above San Vittore on 1 November 1943 just hours before a massive artillery barrage to dislodge the Germans from that locale. The town's structures comprised a pile of rubble after the bombardment through which American infantry searched for any remaining enemy soldiers. Throughout the entire campaign, heights such as this one provided positions to direct artillery fire on locales and troops movements below. (*NARA*)

(**Above**) A British Eighth Army Bren-gun team is situated amid the snow-capped peaks between the Sangro and Moro rivers in late December 1943. This gun's duo comprised an observation post to report on German movements in the valleys below their perch. In this difficult terrain, which precluded rapid advances and flanking manoeuvres, the Germans fielded the 16th and 26th Panzer, the 29th Panzergrenadier and the 1st Parachute divisions all grouped into LXXVI Panzer Corps. Montgomery ordered Dempsey's XIII Corps to advance on the left flank while the main attack was to be delivered by Allfrey's V Corps along the Adriatic coast. The Eighth Army infantry divisions eventually included the British 78th, the Indian 8th, the 1st Canadian and the 2nd New Zealand, as the British 5th Division was moved to the Garigliano River Front. (*NARA*)

(**Opposite, above**) British Eighth Army infantrymen are shown descending a steep slope in single file towards a typical Italian village with numerous dwellings after fierce fighting with the Germans there. In addition to the imposing terrain, the Germans often fortified the masonry houses with machine-guns and mortars necessitating direct assault or bombardment to evict the Nazis. (*NARA*)

(**Opposite, below**) An American infantry patrol is seen moving through an olive grove toward Naples after the Salerno Battle ended. Monte Vesuvius is situated in the background while a pair of M1917 0.30-inch calibre water-cooled Browning machine-guns (*right*) covered the advance. Much of the Salerno Plain's battlefield terrain inland from the beaches was farmland broken up by vineyards, orchards, irrigation ditches and creek tributaries. Enemy mortars, artillery and machine-guns fired on troop movements in the open, even in a concealed grove, in addition to enemy landmines having been sown. (*NARA*)

Three British infantrymen in the 8th Battalion, Royal Fusiliers of British X Corps are shown crawling on their bellies through the mire of a sugar cane field near the Volturno River in October 1943. The unit's movement was prone to being observed in the open from the hills above. (*NARA*)

A British infantryman is shown peering around the corner of a stone building in an Italian town on the alert for a concealed Nazi sniper or machine-gun nest situated in a window or doorway beyond. (*NARA*)

Members of a British Eighth Army infantry section are shown advancing past the shuttered windows of an Italian village's stone houses. From the lip of a shell hole (*right foreground*), a Bren-gun team provided cover. (*NARA*)

British infantrymen are shown marching in single file past a church's tall steeple. Direct observation of one's enemy was advantageous for accurate sniper fire, registering of mortar and artillery rounds and notification of troop movements. *(NARA)*

British soldiers of the Royal Fusiliers, part of the 56th (London) Infantry Division, are shown manning an observation post (OP) near Battipaglia on D-Day +1 at Salerno as it was involved in the spotting for Allied field artillery and naval gunfire to bombard enemy positions in the railway hub along the Tusciano River. After a brief British occupation, Battipaglia was to remain in German hands until 18 September 1943. *(NARA)*

A British X Corps rifleman is shown taking aim at enemy positions in a bomb-ravaged Italian town on the Garigliano River Front in mid-December 1943. Ruins and rubble served as excellent sites for enemy snipers and machine-gun nests, which delayed the advance of Allied units. Part of the Gustav Line was situated on the Garigliano River as it flowed into the Gulf of Gaeta to the south of Minturno. (NARA)

A sign cautioned British troops to take Mepacrine anti-malarial tablets on posted days and to apply anti-mosquito cream after sunset. Southern Italy was rife with mosquitoes that transmitted malaria. On Sicily, British troops suffered from a malaria outbreak that resulted in an estimated eighty-three hospital admissions per 1,000 troops, principally due to drug shortages and reluctance to use the cream. Also, due to the heat, soldiers had their tunic sleeves rolled up and wore short pants. *(NARA)*

An Allied soldier is shown leading his sure-footed pack mule up a steep rocky slope in order to re-supply other members of his unit. The white tape in the background served as a night-time guide to minimise falling. The mountainous terrain necessitated use of pack animals as roads for vehicles were often absent. *(NARA)*

An Eighth Army Canadian 1st Division infantryman wore a reversible hooded Parka with the camouflage white side out for the winter snow of early 1944 on the Adriatic coast of Italy. A fierce winter gripped the Apennine Mountains, beginning on 10 November 1943 with torrential cold rains, floods and snowstorms. The Apennine Mountains run up Italy as a central spine being twice as far from the western coast as from the Adriatic one. The two Allied armies east and west of the Apennines were effectively fighting separate wars. *(NARA)*

British sappers atop a watering truck attempted to keep the road surface wet along the coastal plain on Italy's Tyrrhenian coast during the late summer to minimise dust. German observers, after seeing dust clouds, assumed that a motorised column was in transit and ordered artillery shelling of the road. A sign standing at the side of the road warned, 'Slow, Dust Brings Shells'. *(NARA)*

American engineers are shown detonating explosive charges to destroy German roadblocks as the enemy retreated from Salerno to the Volturno River, north of Naples, in late September 1943. (*NARA*)

(**Opposite, above**) British X Corps sappers and tankers used brute force to move massive triangle-shaped concrete barriers that served as obstacles to the British 7th Armoured Division. Tanks advanced north from Naples to the Volturno River in the vicinity of Grazzanise in early October 1943. (*NARA*)

(**Opposite, below**) Near Cancello, on British X Corps' advance towards Capua and the Volturno River barrier, infantrymen of the 56th Division are seen racing across a railway bridge partially destroyed by the retreating Germans in early October 1943. Nazi bridge infrastructure destruction delayed the Allied river crossings and compelled their units' engineers to work arduously building temporary structures to enable infantry, vehicles, and armour to cross waterways, such as the Volturno River. (*NARA*)

(**Above**) US VI Corps Infantry are shown pulling the rope of a hastily constructed ferry to bring their wooden assault boat across the rain-swollen Volturno River, which was an excellent waterway obstacle to defend at flood stage in October 1943. The river arose in the mountains near Isernia and descended south-westward towards Venafro. The watercourse then turned south-east and paralleled the Tyrrhenian coast for roughly 30 miles. Near the village of Amorosi, the Volturno was conjoined by the waters of the Calore River. From Amorosi, the river turned south-westward and flowed towards Castel Volturno on the Tyrrhenian coast, through such locales as Capua and Grazzanise, which were to be assault points for the British 56th Infantry and 7th Armoured divisions, respectively. The meandering path of the Volturno River would necessitate successive crossings of this waterway during the US VI Corps advance north of Caserta. (*NARA*)

(**Above**) British X Corps Royal Engineers of the 272nd Field Company are shown pulling the ropes to move their wooden ferry situated atop pontoon boats. To the sappers' right, infantrymen in Universal carriers prepare to disembark on the far shore of the Volturno River in mid-October 1943 near Castel Volturno, which was located on the coastal road near the Tyrrhenian coast. (*NARA*)

(**Opposite**) At a destroyed stone bridge site (*background*), US engineers are shown completing their construction of an invaluable Bailey Bridge. Devised by a British War Office civilian, Donald Bailey, these temporary, 10-foot pre-fabricated steel truss bridge sections were transported to river crossings or demolished bridge sites for rapid assembly with simple tools. After a road surface of wood planking was added to the newly erected structure, it was pushed out across the span to be bridged. Bailey Bridges were able to support a minimum of 20 tons of matériel to cross a waterway. Allied Forces headquarters projected a need for 1,000 Bailey Bridges to span the waterways throughout the Italian Peninsula to the Po River in the north. However, Allied engineers ultimately built 3,000 temporary Bailey Bridge spans in less than two years for a total distance of roughly 60 miles. (*NARA*)

(**Above**) A steel treadway bridge situated on pontoons came apart during the Volturno River in flood stage in October 1943. The structure had been erected by the US 16th Engineer Battalion of the 1st Armoured Division. The Volturno River rose to 18 feet in ten hours of torrential autumn rains and swept away many temporary bridges. (*NARA*)

(**Opposite, above**) An M4 medium tank of the 4th County of London Yeomanry of the 7th Armoured Division in British X Corps is shown climbing the steep bank of the far shore of the Volturno River after fording the waterway near Grazzanise in mid-October 1943. Note the wading exhaust tanks situated in the rear of the armoured vehicle adapted for the river crossing. The armoured crossing occurred between the river assaults made by the British 46th Division just to the east of Castel Volturno and the British 56th Division near Capua. (*NARA*)

(**Opposite, below**) A British Jeep attempted to ford a flooded stream near Caserta, just to the south-east of Capua, after the retreating Germans demolished a bridge over the waterway. This was commonplace for Fifth Army troops trying to traverse rain-swollen Italian rivers and streams at flood stage as insufficient Bailey Bridge sections existed to span all the waterways' requisite crossing points. (*NARA*)

(**Opposite, above**) A British truck is shown pulling a smaller one out of a mud hole with other vehicles (*background*) lined up to similarly attempt time-consuming manoeuvring down the small stream's mired bank. 'General Mud', like the mountainous terrain, was a Nazi force multiplier, who held its defensive positions long enough on the Volturno River Front to enable Kesselring to complete the Gustav Line's more permanent concrete and steel positions for the upcoming winter battles. (*NARA*)

(**Above**) Fifth Army sappers are shown laying a log or 'corduroy' road through a muddy ravine near Teano, halfway between the Volturno and Garigliano rivers, ravaged by autumn rains in November 1943. The Germans had defended the British 56th Division advance near Teano with their hastily constructed field works along the Barbara Line, which ran from Monte Massico near the west coast through the villages of Teano and Presenzano and then into the Matese Mountains. (*NARA*)

(**Opposite, below**) American fighter pilots were driven in a utility truck to their waiting aircraft to commence an air cover sortie to neutralise enemy positions for Allied assault troops. The makeshift beachhead airfield lacked an all-weather surface. The numerous small craters and ubiquitous mud made landings and take-offs hazardous. Also, these airstrips were often shelled by German artillery. (*NARA*)

An American engineer is shown assembling perforated steel matting strips (Marston Matting) for a fighter airstrip. A single piece of this steel planking weighed over 60lb and was 10ft long by 15in wide. Developed in the US before the war, the term 'Marston Matting' was derived from Marston, North Carolina, adjacent to the Camp Mackall airfield where the material was initially utilised on the runway there. A 200ft-wide by 5,000ft-long runway could be constructed by a small team of engineers within two days. (NARA)

(**Opposite, above**) A British infantryman is inspecting a dug-in, shell-pocked Nazi tank turret that served as a fixed fortification against the Allied Fifth Army northern advance after the successful Salerno invasion. Although natural terrain features, such as the Volturno River, provided excellent obstacles to defend, Kesselring was busy constructing more fortified positions, such as this one, to the north along what would be called the Winter Line. (NARA)

(**Opposite, below**) Two American Military Policemen are shown guarding a camouflaged Nazi artillery fortification that was situated atop a concrete slab. Some German steel pillboxes were smaller and even portable as enemy efforts to construct Nazi fortification lines had to be hasty to keep pace with the continuing Allied advance. (NARA)

An open cistern served as a German MG 42 infantry position in the Gustav Line defences at Monte Cassino in late 1943. Field Marshal Kesselring, while searching for suitable lines of defence to delay the Allied northward advance, discovered the natural strength of the terrain at Cassino, just across the Rapido River, 70 miles to Rome's south. In October 1943, Hitler sided with Kesselring's plan to defend the Cassino massif in strength. In order to man the Gustav Line's defences, Hitler dispatched two infantry divisions and some artillery from northern Italy, previously under Rommel's command. (NARA)

(**Opposite, above**) A British X Corps infantryman, armed with a Thompson sub-machine-gun, captured a surrendering Nazi position beneath a footpath in an Italian town during the Fifth Army advance from Naples to the Volturno River in early October 1943. The British 46th Infantry, 7th Armoured and 56th Infantry divisions were moving along a west-to-east line from Castel Volturno near the Tyrrhenian Sea cost to Capua, just south of the Volturno River to the north-west of Caserta. British X Corps reached the Volturno by 5 October without much difficulty, but met strong resistance from the German 15th Panzer Grenadier and the Hermann Göring divisions between Capua and the coast. The Nazi defence at Capua was stout as one of the two main roads to Rome emanated from there: Highway 6, which coursed through the town north-westward and crossed the Rapido River at Cassino. Highway 7 ran along the coast and crossed the Garigliano River near Minturno. (NARA)

(**Opposite, below**) American infantrymen with a rocket launcher, the bazooka, are shown taking aim against a Nazi position sequestered behind the thick masonry walls of an Italian cathedral during the winter of 1943. The bazooka was a recoilless weapon introduced into combat during the Tunisian campaign and had a range of 300 yards, but for accuracy the target was usually within 100 yards. The weapon had a two-man crew and fired a high-explosive anti-tank projectile that was used against enemy armour as well as pillboxes, sniper redoubts or artillery observers in church steeples, or other enemy positions that were difficult to get close to neutralise. (NARA)

(**Above**) The Fiocche Tobacco Factory was situated just to the north of the Sele River near Persano and became a major battleground during the combat at Salerno. On 11 September 1943, advancing elements of the US 45th Infantry Division encountered this circular building that the enemy turned into a fortress. The Tobacco Factory changed sides several times throughout the Salerno conflict. (*USAMHI*)

(**Opposite, above**) In mid-December 1943, British X Corps troops from the 56th Infantry Division took shelter in their shallow dugouts in the Monte Camino sector during the Fifth Army advance towards Cassino, 16 miles to the north-west, through the Mignano Gap. The German Bernhardt Line, a temporary line of defences, ran here from the southern end of the Barbara Line at Mondragone on the Tyrrhenian coast eastward towards the Mignano Gap to the west of the Garigliano River between Montes Santa Croce and Camino. On 6 November, the British 56th Division attacked Monte Camino from the south while the US 3rd Division assaulted it from the east. Both Allied attacks against the German XIV Panzer Corps defenders failed to break through the Mignano Gap and the Allied commanders called for a halt in the operations in such harsh terrain and deplorable weather. (*NARA*)

(**Opposite, below**) A US VI Corps forward 0.30-inch calibre Browning machine-gun outpost is shown after having been dug-out from open ground and covered with earth, corrugated steel and some minor camouflage. Temporary fortifications such as these were constructed soon after amphibious landings to establish a perimeter's edge to detect an enemy counter-attack. (*NARA*)

(**Opposite, above**) On the Sangro River Front, troops from the British 78th Infantry Division, which were veterans of both North Africa and Sicily, kept watch on the northern bank of the river from openings in an Italian farm's outbuilding in late November 1943. The British 78th Division reached the Sangro River on 8 November after the German 16th Panzer Division withdrew to fortifications above the river's northern bank. (*NARA*)

(**Opposite, below**) A Military Policeman (MP) in the US 34th Infantry Division is shown directing traffic from a roadside dugout covered partially by some wooden fence material north of Cassino on 27 January 1944. This division's three regiments, the 133rd, 135th and 168th, were tasked in early 1944 with crossing the Rapido River opposite Caira and Monte Castellone. The 34th Division was to be assisted by the 142nd Infantry Regiment of the 36th Division, which had not been committed to the more southerly, disastrous Rapido River crossing of 20–22 January. German counter-attacks by the 44th Infantry Division ultimately prevented the Americans from seizing Cassino and the Benedictine abbey from this northern attack route. (*NARA*)

(**Above**) Royal Artillery (RA) gunners from a field regiment are shown exiting the bomb shelter that they constructed against Nazi shelling and air-raids. The *Luftwaffe* harassed the Allied beachheads constantly with fighter-bombers, medium bombers and radio-controlled glider bombs. (*NARA*)

An American engineer is shown probing soft sand for land mines with his bayonet near a barbed-wire obstacle on one of the assault beachheads. The bayonet was handled at a low diagonal angle in order to not accidentally depress the pressure sensor and detonate the mine. The German 'S' (*Schrapnellmine*) mine or Bouncing Betty had its standard pressure sensor activated by approximately 15lb or greater of weight, so that animals or debris would not prematurely detonate it. (*NARA*)

(**Opposite, above**) Royal Artillery (RA) signalers are shown taking cover in a deep foxhole after the German counter-attack commenced. Along the Salerno assault beaches, signals detachments were vital to pinpoint enemy armour and troop concentrations in order to co-ordinate Allied naval gunfire to defend the beachhead's perimeter. (*NARA*)

(**Opposite, below**) Once the Allied invasion forces were ashore, one of the tasks was to situate fighter aircraft within the beachhead to provide both air cover and to conduct fighter-bomber missions on German ground targets in support of the infantry. An Allied fighter aircraft is shown being moved by its ground crew into a revetment constructed from large sand-filled wine casks and sandbags around such an improvised airfield. (*NARA*)

Two Canadian sappers are shown locating German *Tellermines* with a metal mine detector and then digging them out of the road surface manually in order to de-fuse them. *Teller* is German for dish, which described the shape of the typical land mines for tanks and light vehicles. (*NARA*)

(**Opposite, above**) Several British Eighth Army sappers in Calabria are shown in a line abreast of one another probing an area that had been identified as a minefield. The sappers were using long steel rods carefully inserted into the ground at a low diagonal angle to avoid detonation of the devices. The process was time-consuming as metal detectors were not always available. Axis landmines and booby traps were numerous and were to both delay the Allied advance and inflict demoralising casualties as the inland advance proceeded slowly against the retreating German 26th Panzer and 29th Panzer Grenadier divisions towards the Salerno battlefield. (*NARA*)

(**Opposite, below**) An example of a German anti-tank (AT) *Tellermine* is shown as it was gently pulled out of the ground safely in order to remove the detonator on the base of the planted landmine. The typical AT mine detonated with 350lb pressure. It was 12 inches wide and 3 inches high. Because of its rather high operating pressure to set off the fuse, only a vehicle or heavy object passing over the mine would set it off. The *Tellermine* was capable of blasting the tracks off any Allied tank or destroying a lightly armoured vehicle. Some mines had a booby trap inside the mine itself. Any attempt to disarm the mine by unscrewing the pressure plate or the screw cap to remove the fuse often automatically detonated the *Tellermine*. (*NARA*)

A German 'S' (*Schrapenellmine*) is shown above. When detonated, this device rose to about 5 feet in the air and exploded sending steel-ball-shrapnel flying in all directions, as to inflict casualties on unshielded Allied infantrymen in their upper torso and head regions. These devices were usually 5 inches high and weighed about 9lb, containing over 6oz of explosive charge. This 'S' mine was discovered by this Canadian sapper concealed under a piece of roof tiling with its trip-wire attached to a door. (*NARA*)

Two American infantrymen are shown walking carefully between two markers denoting a path that was cleared of mines by engineers. An 'S' mine (*right foreground*) that had probably been de-fused is hanging on some wire. (*NARA*)

(**Opposite, above**) A British sniper on the Cassino Front in December 1943 is shown with his No. 4 Mk I(T) Short Magazine Lee-Enfield (SMLE) rifle with a sniper's No. 32 telescopic sight, detachable cheek-rest, and a special leather sling. It was an effective combination to counter the ever-present German snipers. (*NARA*)

(**Opposite, below**) A Canadian infantryman is shown loading his Projector Infantry Anti-Tank (PIAT) Mk 1 weapon in Ortona on the Adriatic coast in December 1943. A PIAT was usually assigned to a two-man team and made its combat debut on Sicily. It was designed in 1942 when the British needed an effective, inexpensive portable AT weapon for infantrymen. The weapon's design was based on the spigot mortar system that launched a 2.5lb bomb using a spring and a cartridge in the tail of the projectile. The weight of the PIAT was 32lb unloaded and had an operational range of 115 yards for direct fire against armoured vehicles and 350 yards in an indirect fire mode against bunkers or fortified houses. The PIAT was able to deliver its charge with the force of a 75mm AT gun. In theory, the PIAT's bomb was able to pierce up to 4in of armour. However, field experience on Sicily and in Italy refuted that claim of penetrating ability. There was no muzzle smoke to give away the location of the crew, although there was a powerful recoil and some difficulty in cocking the spring mechanism. (*NARA*)

(**Above**) British mortarmen of an infantry brigade support group are shown adjusting the tube on their relatively new M2 4.2in mortar. This heavy mortar, with its 105lb 4ft rifled tube, was designed to hurl a 20lb bomb from 560 to 4,400 yards. This weapon was used effectively on the Italian mainland since it delivered high explosive shells in the rough mountainous terrain where rounds were fired onto enemy positions along reverse slopes with plunging bombardment rather than direct fire. Also, it was extremely difficult to transport more cumbersome field artillery pieces into the mountains. (*USAMHI*)

(**Above**) A Royal Artillery (RA) crew is shown firing its QF, 3.7in heavy anti-aircraft (AA) gun in an uncharacteristic field artillery manner in November 1943. There was much argument over the refusal to use this weapon in a counter-battery, counter-mortar, or anti-tank (AT) capacity as the Germans deployed their dual-purpose 88-mm FLAK. Nonetheless, the 3.7in guns were used effectively in an AT role, but sparingly, against Panzers in North Africa. These 3.7in guns were also used, as shown, in a field artillery role quite extensively in the second half of the war on the Italian mainland, north-west Europe, Burma and the south-west Pacific. (*NARA*)

(**Opposite, above**) A Royal Artillery (RA) crew has prepared to fire a BL 4.5in medium field cannon (not to be confused with the QF, 4.5in Howitzer or QF, 4.5in anti-aircraft gun) in defence of the Allied bridgehead. The earlier Mk 1 was first issued in 1938 and equipped the RA in northern France. Issues of the Mk 2 ordnance, which shared a common carriage with the BL 5.5in medium field cannon, started in 1941. Both British and Canadian gunners utilised this artillery piece effectively on the Italian mainland. (*NARA*)

(**Opposite, below**) A Royal Artillery (RA) crew is shown loading a shell into the breach of their BL 5.5in Mk 2 medium field cannon at Axis forces. The Mk 2 was on a new carriage that was also used with the BL 4.5-inch gun. This artillery piece was first introduced into the British Army in May 1942 to replace the 6-inch Howitzer, and it was deployed in the North African campaign. With a new high explosive (HE) shell that was 20lb lighter, the maximum range of the gun improved considerably to just over 9 miles. (*NARA*)

(**Opposite, above**) An American 155 M1 Howitzer crew is shown firing on German positions in the area north of Salerno area in late September 1943. It was specifically designed to be towed by a motorised vehicle and, as shown, had a split trail mount and gun shield. It fired a 95lb shell a maximum range of over 16,000 yards. (*NARA*)

(**Opposite, below**) A plume of fire is seen emanating from the barrel of a 155mm Long Tom M2 cannon concealed by some hessian camouflage netting and vegetation. This artillery piece was one of the most important weapons in the US Army's long-range artillery inventory during the Second World War and, interestingly, was based on a French design used during the First World War. The Long Tom's carriage with its ten wheels (eight on its gun mount and two on the trail mount) was specially designed to augment cross-country movement. It had a maximum range of over 25,000 yards and fired one 200lb round per minute. (*USAMHI*)

(**Above**) A 240mm Howitzer, nicknamed the Black Dragon, of the US VI Corps' 97th Field Artillery Battalion, is shown under camouflage netting being made ready for firing against German positions in the Mignano Gap area in late December 1943. This artillery piece was the most powerful weapon deployed by US Field Artillery units in the Second World War. It fired a 360lb high explosive shell and was designed for use against heavily reinforced targets such as the Germans had situated atop many of the mountains south of Cassino. (*USAMHI*)

(**Opposite, above**) British Commandos are shown disembarking from a Royal Navy landing craft. They were equipped with special lightweight folding bicycles with extra loads attached to the handlebars. Bicycles were used by signalers as well as dispatch riders in British Airborne and Commando units to enhance mobility in order to facilitate communication once arriving at designated targets before heavier vehicles, such as Jeeps could be off-loaded. (*NARA*)

(**Opposite, below**) A Universal carrier is shown with its Bren-gun mounted on a monopod for anti-aircraft (AA) use. In addition, the four-man crew had installed a captured Italian 20mm anti-tank (AT). Intriguingly, the utilisation of the AT gun was reminiscent of the Boys AT rifle which fired a .55in bullet, that had been part of the armament of Universal carriers. However, it was inadequate against enemy armour even during the early part of the war and was phased out. Other ordnance to replace the Boys AT rifle included Vickers medium machine-guns, 2in and 3in mortars, and the Projector Infantry Anti-Tank (PIAT) weapon. (*NARA*)

(**Above**) An American M8 light armoured car with a 37mm turret gun and a .50-inch calibre Browning heavy machine-gun is shown near Cassino. The M8, with its four-man crew, was widely used by all Allied nations and was dubbed the Greyhound by the British. The vehicle's strengths included cross-country manoeuvrability, a road speed of 55mph, its firepower, and a low silhouette for concealment. (*USAMHI*)

An Eighth Army 40mm Bofors anti-aircraft (AA) gun on its mobile platform is shown in action in the mountains along the Adriatic coast in November 1943. This weapon was designed for the Swedish Navy in the mid-1930s and was subsequently manufactured by other nations. The gun was ideally suited for its AA role firing 120 rounds per minute. This gun had a single-barrel gun on a mobile mounting for land use, while, for naval use, a dual configuration barrel was manufactured. Approximately 2,000lb in weight, this AA gun, although vehicle-towed, was highly mobile. (*NARA*)

(**Opposite, above**) An American M3 half-track is shown with its crew firing its 75mm gun at German positions at Salerno. This armoured vehicle was termed the M3 Gun Mounted Carriage (GMC) and was the primary American heavy tank destroyer in combat during 1942–1943. It suffered from a very limited traverse and its cross-country speed was deemed inadequate. The 75mm gun was of First World War vintage, utilising the French M1897 design. Nonetheless, this M3 GMC was an improvement over its vastly inferior predecessor, the M6 37mm GMC. (*NARA*)

(**Opposite, below**) An American M10 3in-gun motor carriage (GMC) or tank destroyer (TD) of the 601st TD Battalion is shown in the vicinity of an empty enemy pillbox. The M10 saw its combat debut in Tunisia in March 1943 at El Guettar. The TD battalions helped stop 10th Panzer Division armour. The M10 3in GMC was basically an M4A2 medium tank chassis mounting a 3in M7 gun, which had been developed as an anti-aircraft (AA) weapon, in an open turret. It was a marked improvement over the M3 half-track-mounted armoured vehicles and became the standard TD throughout Tunisia and into the Italian campaign. (*USAMHI*)

(**Above**) A towed British Eighth Army 17-pounder anti-tank (AT) is shown manoeuvring out of thick mud on the Sangro River Front in late November 1943. This weapon was one of the best AT guns as it incorporated the newly designed armour-piercing, discarding sabot (APDS) along with conventional armour-piercing (AP) and high explosive (HE) ammunition. The 17-pounder was initially deployed in Tunisia to combat the German Mk VI Tiger tank. (*NARA*)

(**Opposite, above**) American soldiers of an M7 105mm Howitzer motor carriage (HMC) of Battery A, 69th Armoured Field Artillery Battalion of the US 1st Armored Division are seen in bivouac. This self-propelled artillery (SPA) vehicle was called a Priest by the British because of its pulpit-shaped .50-inch calibre machine-gun turret in the front. The Priest first saw combat with British Eighth Army at the Second Battle of El Alamein in October–November 1942. The M7 was built on the M3 medium tank chassis and had a crew of five. (*NARA*)

(**Opposite, below**) A British self-propelled 25-pounder field gun of the 7th Armoured Division, called the Bishop, is shown firing at German positions in night combat at Grazzanise on the Volturno River Front in mid-October 1943. In 1941, the British needed an armoured vehicle to mount their 25-pounder gun for mobility. The Valentine tank chassis was chosen by armour developers and the Bishop became part of Britain's self-propelled artillery (SPA) armamentarium as the British 6- and 17-pounder anti-tank (AT) cannons replaced the 25-pounder field artillery gun as the primary effective AT weapons. (*Author's Collection*)

A British soldier is shown alongside the empty casing of a *Luftwaffe* anti-personnel cluster bomb, AB500-1, which was to release over a score of delayed-action smaller SD-10 devices against Allied troops dug in along the beachhead (*USAMHI*).

(**Opposite, above**) British tankers and infantry inspect a captured French 155mm artillery cannon that had been used by the Germans to shell Allied shipping offshore. This outdated First World War French artillery cannon was the basis for the American Long Tom 155mm gun US Army Ordnance developers in the 1930s due to the cannon's effectiveness during the First World War. (*NARA*)

(**Opposite, below**) American soldiers sitting atop an armoured railcar in the Caserta railway station north-east of Naples. The railcar had been a gift from Hitler to Mussolini and was armed with a quadruple-mounted 20mm *Flakvierling* 38 anti-aircraft (AA) gun, which entered service in 1940 and proved to be one of the most effective German light AA weapons. A 37mm *Flakvierling* 43 did not enter service until 1944. (*NARA*)

(**Above**) A Canadian 1st Division infantryman is seen inspecting a disabled German 75mm Pak 40 anti-tank (AT) gun at Reggio di Calabria soon after Operation Baytown's landings in early September 1943. This Nazi field-gun was developed in late 1939 to counter the development of new heavily armoured Russian tanks and replaced the previously deployed 50mm Pak 38. The major advantages of the 75mm Pak 40 weapon was its high muzzle velocity and excellent range, but its mobility was limited due to heavy weight. (*NARA*)

(**Opposite, above**) An almost 70-ton disabled German 88mm self-propelled gun (SPG) or tank destroyer, called *Ferdinand* after its designer Ferdinand Porsche, is shown after being abandoned by the Nazis in the wake of the British Eighth Army advance in early 1944. This SPG was designed by Porsche in 1942–43 with less than a hundred being built. After a hurried development, the vast majority of these SPGs was first deployed at the Battle of Kursk (German offensive 5 July–16 July 1943) on the Russian Front with an extremely high killing ratio of roughly 10:1 with the range of its 88mm gun. However, it was extremely vulnerable to Soviet infantry placing explosive charges, since the German SPG lacked a machine-gun for defence as well as turret visibility to observe enemy movements. Its slow speed and large size also made it an easy target for Russian gunners. Finally, mechanical failure was a primary reason for these mammoth SPGs becoming disabled. In September 1943, all surviving *Ferdinands* from the Kursk battlefield were withdrawn to Italy. They were fitted with a ball-mounted MG34 in the hull's front for protection against enemy infantry as well as a commander's cupola (*seen above*) for improved vision. This modified *Ferdinand* was renamed the *Elefant*. In Italy, these SPGs were ineffective due to ongoing mechanical failures, their massive weight limiting them from most Italian roads and bridges. (*NARA*)

Canadian infantrymen holding a general purpose MG34 German machine-gun with ammunition belts after capturing an enemy position. The MG34 was an air-cooled, belt-fed weapon that fired a 0.3-inch calibre (7.92mm) round. The *Wehrmacht* had been developing a machine-gun in 1929 that was lighter than the ones used in the First World War but would still have a devastating fire-power effect. Although the MG34 was introduced in 1934, its mass production began two years later, proving to be both expensive and requiring excessive amounts of time for manufacture. It was classified as a light-machine-gun (LMG), weighing just over 25lb with its bipod. However, in more fixed positions could utilise a heavier tripod. Its effective range was over 1,300 yards. The MG34 was widely used by German infantry during the initial years of the war until the later release of the MG42. *(NARA)*

Canadian soldiers examining a pair of German *Nebelwerfers* (Smoke Launcher) in the mountainous region along Highway 17 on the Adriatic Front. During the war, the *Wehrmacht* used a large number of artillery weapons firing rocket-propelled ammunition. These 21cm *Nebelwerfer* 42 weapons launched rocket-propelled projectiles from all five tubes within eight seconds. (*NARA*)

Chapter Three

Commanders and Combatants

Following the thirty-eight-day conquest of Sicily, the Allied commanders in the MTO realised that Italy was not to be a major priority to fight the Nazis, as the United Kingdom was to be the site to concentrate the preponderance of troops and war matériel for an eventual cross-Channel invasion of north-west Europe over the beaches of Normandy. Even prior to the Sicilian campaign, at the Casablanca Conference in January 1943, Allied leaders grappled with the operational planning for utilisation of the accumulated island forces after Messina's successful capture. The main aims of an Allied invasion of the Italian mainland were to divert the maximum number of Nazi forces away from north-west Europe and the Russian Front after Italy's surrender.

For the assaults on the Italian mainland, Operations Baytown, Avalanche and Slapstick, General Dwight D. Eisenhower served again as overall commander-in-chief, Allied Mediterranean Forces with General Harold Alexander as his deputy commander-in-chief and Commanding General, 15th Army Group. The two Allied armies for the amphibious attacks were the US Fifth Army, commanded by Lieutenant-General Mark W. Clark, and the British Eighth Army, commanded by Lieutenant-General Bernard L. Montgomery. Allied naval support for Operation Avalanche was under the command of the experienced US Navy's vice-admiral, Kent K. Hewitt.

The Fifth Army attacking at Salerno comprised two corps: the British X Corps, led by Lieutenant-General Richard L. McCreery, and the US VI Corps, commanded by Major-General Ernest J. Dawley. McCreery's British X Corps fielded the 46th Oak Tree (commanded by Major-General John L.T. Hawkesworth) and the 56th London (commanded by Major-General Douglas A.H. Graham) divisions. The assaulting infantry divisions of the US VI Corps were the 36th Texas (commanded by Major-General Fred Walker), and the 45th Thunderbirds (commanded by Major-General Troy Middleton). Fifth Army reserve formations on Sicily included the US 3rd Infantry Division, commanded by Major-General Lucian Truscott, and the US 82nd Airborne Division, led by Major-General Matthew B. Ridgway. The British 7th Armoured Division was to come ashore on the fifth or sixth day of the invasion.

Specialised formations for Operation Avalanche landings included three US ranger battalions (1st, 2nd and 4th rangers), under the command of Colonel William O. Darby and the British Special Service Brigade, led by Brigadier Robert Laycock. The latter unit comprised the British Army's No. 2 and Royal Marines' No. 41 Commandos. These elite Allied formations were to spearhead the ambitious Allied plans north of the Sele River by gaining possession and holding the mountain passes north of Maiori and Vietri between the town of Salerno to the east and the Sorrento Peninsula to the west. The British and Royal Marine Commandos were to also aid in the capture of the port of Salerno, thereby assisting the two British infantry divisions in their mission to seize the Montecorvino airfield and possess the road and rail centre of Battipaglia. As Spitfires of the Royal Air Force, based on Sicily, were capable of operating only as far as Salerno and, with an extra fuel tank, patrol over the beachhead for only ten-to-twenty minutes, the Montecorvino airfield was a vital Allied objective.

The British Eighth Army was tasked with crossing the Strait of Messina onto the toe of Italy, Operation Baytown on 3 September 1943. The attacking force, British XIII Corps under Lieutenant-General Miles Dempsey, comprised the Canadian 1st (led by Major-General Guy Simonds) and British 5th (commanded by Major-General Gerard Bucknall) divisions. Both were veteran formations from the Sicily campaign. XIII Corps was to be supported by the 1st Canadian Army Armoured Brigade.

For Operation Slapstick – an amphibious assault on 9 September tasked with the capture of Taranto and Brindisi, the latter on the Adriatic coast – the British 1st Airborne Division was employed. This formation was under the command of Major-General George F. Hopkinson, who was mortally wounded on 9 September and replaced by Major-General Ernest Down. Since the available Allied airlift was sufficient for the eventual airborne transport of only one division, the US 82nd Airborne still on Sicily, the British 1st Airborne Division was chosen for the seaborne assault on Taranto.

Additional strength for the subsequent British operations on the Adriatic coast was in the form of the British 78th Division in Sicily and the Indian 8th Division in Egypt under the headquarters command of Lieutenant-General Charles Allfrey's British V Corps. The 2nd New Zealand Division, under Lieutenant-General Bernard Freyberg, was also preparing for movement to eastern Italy from areas in the Middle East and north Africa.

Even with the Italian capitulation on 8 September, the Germans were still able to field over 100,000 troops on the Italian mainland. The German top leadership in Italy was initially divided between two strong-willed field marshals, Albert Kesselring (commander-in-chief, Army Group South) and Erwin Rommel (commander-in-chief, Army Group B), who were often at odds with one another. Originally, Hitler favoured Rommel's plan to hold the north of Italy in the Northern Apennines after the Italian government's surrender. However, in mid-November, the Nazi leader transferred Rommel to France, leaving Kesselring in sole command as commander-in-chief Army Group C to wage his defensive battle against the two Allied armies south of Rome.

At Salerno, the Allies were to face German General Heinrich von Vietinghoff, commanding general of the Nazi Tenth Army. Out of communication with Kesselring on 9 September 1943, when Operation Avalanche was commencing, Vietinghoff decided to repel the invaders at the Salerno beachhead rather than withdraw his forces to the north. Days before, he had chosen to evacuate his forces from Calabria and the heel of Italy around Brindisi and Taranto in order to bring those units together with other ones converging around Salerno. The withdrawing German formations from the south were to delay British Eighth Army's advance and its link-up with the US Fifth Army. Kesselring approved wholeheartedly with Vietinghoff's troop dispositions and desire to contest the Allied landings along the Salerno beaches. In addition, Vietinghoff instituted plans to seize the Italian bases and coastal defences once the Italians formally left as co-belligerents.

Vietinghoff's Tenth Army comprised the XIV and LXXVI Panzer corps under General Hermann Balck and General Traugott Herr, respectively. Balck was acting for General Hans-Valentine Hube, the XIV Corps commander, who was on leave at the time of the Salerno invasion. Both Balck and Herr were experts in tank warfare, having aggressively led smaller formations with initiative on diverse battlefields spanning from Poland, France, Greece, the Balkans and Russia.

The XIV Panzer Corps fielded the 16th Panzer (Lieutenant-General Rudolph Sieckenius), the Hermann Göring (under Major-General Wilhelm Schmalz), and the 15th Panzer Grenadier (under Lieutenant-General Eberhard Rodt) divisions. The 15th Panzer Grenadier Division was stationed near Gaeta and was re-fitting after its combat on Sicily when it was moved to the Salerno area. The Hermann Göring Division was also reforming near Naples after its evacuation from Sicily and regained much of its unit's strength. The only Nazi formation in the immediate vicinity of the Allied amphibious attack at Salerno was the 16th Panzer Division, and that was widely situated along the Tyrrhenian coast on the Salerno Plain at over half-a-dozen defensive zones between Salerno and Agropoli. As such, the 16th Panzer Division alone was to initially absorb the brunt of the Allied invasion around Salerno's environs on 9 September until reinforcements could arrive, principally from the south. Both of Balck's more northerly disposed forces, the 15th Panzer Grenadier and Hermann Göring divisions, were involved in attacks against the Allied elite formations at the Chiunzi and Molina passes at Nocera and Cava, respectively, as well as against the British 46th Division holding Salerno itself.

The LXXVI Panzer Corps was composed of the 26th Panzer (under Lieutenant-General Smilo Freiherr von Lüttwitz), the 3rd Panzer Grenadier (commanded by

Lieutenant-General Fitz-Hubert Grässer) and the 29th Panzer Grenadier (commanded by Lieutenant-General Walter Freis) divisions. The 29th Panzer Grenadier and 26th Panzer divisions were in Calabria at the time of Operation Baytown, the former unit having arrived from Sicily a few weeks earlier after the Messina evacuation. The 26th Panzer Division was stationed in France in a garrison capacity until it was moved to the Italian theatre in June 1943. The 3rd Panzer Grenadier Division had arrived in Italy in June 1943 and was stationed near Rome. It was subsequently ordered south to Naples as the Allied invasion threat loomed following the Axis debacle on Sicily.

By mid-November 1943, other Nazi divisions were to be situated in southern Italy, such as the 94th Infantry Division near Minturno and along the Garigliano River, the 44th Infantry Division in the Monte Cassino sector and the 305th Infantry Division defending from the Isernia area north into the Eighth Army zone on the Sangro River Front. Kesselring was quite adept at reinforcing all of these areas with additional Nazi formations as the two Allied armies were to continue their offensives.

(**Opposite, above**) American president Franklin D. Roosevelt (*left*) and British prime minister Winston S. Churchill (*right*) are shown sitting aboard HMS *Prince of Wales* in Placentia Bay, Newfoundland, in August 1941 for joint services. Behind the two political leaders were: (*l-to-r*) Admiral Ernest King, USN, commander-in-chief, Atlantic Fleet; US Army Chief of Staff General George C. Marshall; and British Chief of the Imperial General Staff (CIGS), General Sir John Dill. Other dignitaries in the background behind King were Harry Hopkins (*left*) and Averill Harriman (*right*). At this Atlantic conference it was decided to reinforce both England and its ally the Soviet Union with American aid, largely through the Lend-Lease, in order to combat the Nazi onslaught. (*NARA*)

(**Opposite, below**) General Dwight D. Eisenhower, Allied Forces Commander, Mediterranean Theatre of Operation (MTO), is shown sitting in the front passenger seat of his Jeep. Lieutenant-General Mark W. Clark, the Fifth Army commanding general, is shown sitting behind him in the rear of the vehicle. Both American generals are seen striking up a friendly conversation with the crew of a heavily laden, camouflage-painted British Universal carrier after the conclusion of the fighting at Salerno during the third week of September 1943. Eisenhower was ceaseless in ensuring co-operation among all Allied combatants and was well-known for sending American officers back stateside for disparaging comments made about the British. (*NARA*)

General Harold Alexander, commanding general of the Allied 15th Army Group, is shown sitting on the left in the rear of a staff car with Major-General Geoffrey Keyes, the future US II Corps commanding general in Italy, on the way to Palermo, Sicily, before Operation Avalanche. Alexander, a favourite of Churchill, had supervised both the Dunkirk and the Burma evacuations in 1940 and 1942, respectively. He then went on to replace General Claude Auchinleck in August 1942 as commander-in-chief, Middle East. There he provided strategic oversight for General Bernard Montgomery's victory at the Second Battle of El Alamein in November 1942. During the six-month Tunisian campaign, Alexander organised and directed fractious Allied commanders under the Allied 18th Army Group. He repeated this leadership role during the thirty-eight-day Sicilian campaign as the head of the Allied 15th Army Group. There he had to again deal with two enormous military egos, those of Lieutenant-General George S. Patton and Montgomery. After the Salerno invasion, Alexander would oversee the tactical and strategic military leadership of General Clark's Fifth and Montgomery's Eighth armies during the Italian Campaign. Early in October, Alexander established his Allied 15th Army Group headquarters near Bari on the Adriatic coast. Alexander received his field marshal's baton on 12 December 1944 to become the Supreme Commander Allied Forces Headquarters in Italy, leaving the 15th Army Group to Clark. As for Keyes, he was Patton's deputy of the US Seventh Army on Sicily and led a provisional corps that was instrumental in the early seizure of Palermo. Keyes was a West Point graduate, a veteran cavalryman, and was regarded as an intellectual soldier. During the approach to the Gustav Line in December 1943–January 1944, Keyes was to be in charge of the US II Corps, comprising the US 34th and 36th Infantry divisions, which were heavily blooded in their Rapido River crossings at the First Battle of Cassino. (USAMHI)

(**Left**) Generals Montgomery (*left*) and Clark (*right*), the British Eighth and US Fifth Army commanding generals, respectively, are shown touring the battlefield after the battle for Salerno ended in late September 1943. Montgomery's veteran Eighth Army, having fought the Axis in Egypt, across Libya and in Tunisia, had just completed a contentious campaign against the Nazis along the eastern coast of Sicily and around the Monte Etna massif. His invasion of the Italian mainland on 3 September with British XIII Corps, Operation Baytown, met with little enemy resistance but much delay as the German 29th Panzer Grenadier and 26th Panzer divisions withdrew from Calabria to the Salerno battlefield. Clark, who was a close associate of Eisenhower and an integral member of the Allied team in north-west Africa, had formed the Fifth Army headquarters in January 1943 and was tasked with planning an amphibious assault on Italy's Tyrrhenian coast in the general vicinity of Naples, Operation Avalanche. After much deliberation among the various Allied leaders and service chiefs, an attack in the Gulf of Salerno was chosen. (*NARA*)

(**Opposite, right**) Lieutenant-General Richard L. McCreery, commanding general of British X Corps in Clark's Fifth Army, is shown. He would be in charge of the British 46th and 56th infantry divisions as well as having US ranger battalions and British Army and Royal Marine Commandos fighting in his sector. McCreery was a former cavalry officer and a former chief-of-staff of General Alexander in the Middle East. He was a vocal critic, among many others, of Clark's consideration of an urgent abandonment of the American VI Corps sector and re-embarkation along the British X Corps Front north of the Sele River on 13 September 1943 in the face of strong Nazi counter-attacks against the beachhead. Animus and distrust between McCreery and Clark would continue throughout the Italian Campaign. (*NARA*)

General Montgomery (*far left*) is shown with his principal commanders along the Adriatic Front in December 1943. From left-to-right are lieutenant-generals Bernard Freyberg (head of the 2nd New Zealand Division), Charles W. Allfrey (British V Corps commanding general), and Miles Dempsey (British XIII Corps commanding general). Freyberg, a decorated First World War veteran, had seen extensive service in the Middle East, Greece, Crete, El Alamein, and around the Mareth Line defences in south-eastern Tunisia, the latter in charge of the New Zealand Corps comprising his 2nd New Zealand Division, British 8th Armoured Brigade and French general Jacques LeClerc's L Force. Allfrey's British V Corps headquarters, after arriving in Italy via the port of Bari, would be in command of the British 78th and 8th Indian Infantry divisions. Allfrey had led British V Corps' three divisions in the British First Army in Tunisia. In north-west Africa, along with the US II Corps and the French XIX Corps, Allfrey's V Corps moved through the Tunisian Dorsals from the west to force Arnim's Axis forces back to Bizerte and Tunis. During the winter of 1944 in Italy, much of the combat east of the Apennines would be left to Allfrey's V Corps. Dempsey, a close associate of Montgomery from Dunkirk and after having been given command of XIII Corps in North Africa in December 1942, commanded British XIII Corps in Sicily and during the successful Operation Baytown invasion of Calabria. His command in the central part of the Italian Peninsula from mid-October onwards comprised the battle-hardened 1st Canadian and British 5th divisions, both veterans of the Sicily Campaign that had landed at Reggio di Calabria. Dempsey left for England with Montgomery at the end of December 1943 to begin assembling his British Second Army headquarters for the upcoming Normandy invasion. (*Author's Collection*)

Lieutenant-General Oliver Leese (*second from left*) became the Eighth Army's commanding general upon Montgomery's departure to England at the end of December 1943. Here he is shown as British XXX Corps commanding general on Sicily, with Major-General Guy G. Simonds, commanding general of the Canadian 1st Division. Leese was a member of the Coldstream Guards and had served and been wounded on the Somme during the First World War. Like many senior officers, he was evacuated from Dunkirk in 1940 prior to being given command of the Guards Armoured Division. Montgomery promoted Leese to lieutenant-general and placed him in charge of XXX Corps, which he commanded at the Second Battle of El Alamein and at the Mareth Line in Tunisia. In August 1943, after Sicily's conquest, Leese returned to England. However, Montgomery brought him to Italy to take over the Eighth Army. Simonds' division participated as part of British XIII Corps' invasion of Reggio di Calabria, Operation Baytown, on 3 September 1943. These Canadian troops became the acknowledged experts in street-fighting after the fierce combat for Ortona on the Adriatic coast in late December 1943. (*NARA*)

Major-General Ernest J. Dawley, commanding general of US VI Corps at Salerno, is shown. Dawley's VI Corps was initially slated for the Sicily invasion. However, Patton wanted the more experienced II Corps headquarters, under Lieutenant-General Omar Bradley. As such, VI Corps was transferred to Clark's new Fifth Army for the Salerno invasion. The US VI Corps at Salerno consisted of a single assault division, the 36th Infantry, as two regiments of the 45th Infantry Division were held on D-Day, 9 September 1943, as a floating reserve. After the near disaster along the VI Corps beachhead on 13 September, Dawley was sent back stateside. His relationship with Clark was rancorous. (NARA)

Major-General John P. Lucas (right) replaced Dawley as the VI Corps commanding general on 20 September 1943. Here he is shown reviewing maps with his chief-of-staff, Colonel Donald Callaway, at his Venafro sector headquarters in December 1943. Lucas was an artilleryman and was to lead the Allied VI Corps through the Italian mountains during the harsh winter months. (NARA)

Lieutenant-General Mark Clark (*left*) is shown with French Expeditionary Corps (FEC) commander General Alphonse Juin in Italy in December 1943. The FEC, comprising the 2nd Moroccan and 3rd Algerian divisions, launched its attacks across the Rapido River during the final week of January 1944 and captured some strategic heights to the north of Cassino. Juin was held in high regard among the senior Allied military leaders as both a tactician and an offensive-minded commander. In the background to the right is Brigadier Theodore Roosevelt, Jr., who had been the assistant division commanding general of the US 1st Infantry Division in north-west Africa and Sicily. After his relief with the division commander, Major-General Terry de la Mesa Allen, after the capture of Troina on Sicily, Roosevelt became liaison officer with the French forces in Italy. (*NARA*)

General Wladyslaw Anders, commanding general of the 2nd Polish Corps, saluting colours with Allied 15th Army group commander General Alexander in Italy. After a horrendous trek from the Soviet Union through Persia to British lines in the Middle East, the Polish soldiers under his command were to assault Cassino after the failure of the initial Fifth Army attack in January 1944. Under his command, Anders' 2nd Polish Corps comprised the 3rd Carpathian and 5th Kresowa divisions supported by the 2nd Polish Armoured Brigade. *(NARA)*

(**Left**) The US 36th Texas Infantry Division's commanding general, Major-General Fred L. Walker, is shown. He was regarded as a highly competent regular army officer. His division was to be the only assaulting one of VI Corps on 9 September 1943 at the start of Operation Avalanche. It was not until D-Day +1 that the 45th Infantry Division's two regimental combat teams landed to assist Walker's force south of the Sele River. Both Clark and Walker had not allowed the naval task force commander Vice-Admiral H. Kent Hewitt to bombard the 36th Division landing beaches. Unfortunately, without the naval gunfire, the tanks, mortars and machine-guns of the German 16th Panzer Division created initial havoc among the lightly armed American infantry storming the beaches. Walker did not greatly admire his superior Clark, especially after the tentative plan to evacuate the VI Corps beachhead during the Nazi counter-attack of 13 September 1943 and the failed Rapido River crossing by his division on 20–22 January 1944. (*NARA*)

(**Centre**) Major-General Troy Middleton, commanding general of the 45th Infantry Division of US VI Corps, is shown. Middleton was a native of Mississippi and served as the executive officer of the US 47th Infantry Regiment, 4th Division during the First World War, becoming the youngest colonel in the American Expeditionary Force (AEF) at the age of 29. He left the army in 1937 to become an official at the Louisiana State University. After Pearl Harbor, he was recalled back to the army as a lieutenant-colonel with the 4th and then 36th Infantry divisions. In 1942, he was a major-general in command of the 45th Division, a national guard unit made up of south-westerners with many native Americans from Oklahoma, Arizona, Colorado and New Mexico. His division had amphibious experience from Sicily's Operation Husky, pushing inland for 7 miles on 10 July 1943, D-Day at Scoglitti. For Operation Avalanche's D-Day, 9 September 1943, two of his three regimental combat teams (RCTs) would be floating reserve, but would be landed the next day to assist the US 36th Division ashore being attacked by the German 16th Panzer Division south of the town of Salerno. Like Dawley and Walker, Middleton became incensed with Clark's scheme to evacuate the VI Corps beachhead on 13 September. He informed the Fifth Army commander, 'Put food and ammunition behind the 45th … we are going to stay here'. (*NARA*)

(**Right**) Major-General Charles Ryder, the commanding general of the US 34th Infantry Division, is shown. Ryder, a native of Kansas, led this division, a national guard unit composed of mid-westerners from North and South Dakota, Iowa and Minnesota, ashore during Operation Torch, which seized Algiers on 8 November 1942. Although elements of Ryder's 34th Division, as part of Keyes' US II Corps, had made it across the Rapido River in late January 1944 and had, indeed, threatened both the town of Cassino and the Benedictine monastery on the heights above with capture, a failure to reinforce the division's regiments brought the First Battle of Cassino to an inopportune conclusion. (*NARA*)

2 E 389

Then Major William O. Darby (*far left*) and Brigadier-General Lucian Truscott, Jr. (*centre left*), the latter in his cavalry boots and distinctive trousers, are shown in Scotland at a British Commando training facility for a battalion of a new specialised force of American infantrymen to be subsequently remembered as Darby's Rangers. Darby was a West Point graduate, who initially started soldiering as an officer in the army's last horse artillery unit. Truscott gave the elite group its moniker from Rogers Rangers, who fought in the pre-Revolutionary American colonies. Darby went on to command the 1st Ranger Battalion, who assaulted French coastal forts at Arzew as part of the Central Task Force's operations to seize Oran. Truscott said of Darby, 'Never in this war have I known a more gallant, heroic officer.' Truscott went on to command the US sub-task force Goalpost that was charged with the capture of the Mehdia-Port Lyautey area to secure the northern flank of the western task force's assault on Morocco's Atlantic coast on 8 November 1942. He then went on to become commanding general of the 3rd Infantry Division and landed his troops at Licata on Sicily's southern shore in July 1943, before trekking off to capture Palermo as part of Major-General Geoffrey Keyes' provisional corps. Darby's Ranger battalions saw extensive combat at Gela with the US 1st Infantry Division on Sicily, and as part of the provisional corps too. At Salerno, Darby's Rangers were utilised in an elite capacity to seize and hold the important heights at the Chiunzi Pass after landing at Maiori to the west of Salerno along the northern coast of the Gulf of Salerno in the British X Corps sector. (*USAMHI*)

Major-General Matthew B. Ridgway, commanding general of the 82nd Airborne Division, is shown reviewing plans with some of this staff officers at Ribera on Sicily. The 82nd division had a stellar history, having fought in a regular infantry capacity in the First World War in the Meuse-Argonne and at St Mihiel. The infantry division was reactivated in 1942, when it was commanded by Major-General Omar Bradley. It was selected to become the first of the new airborne divisions and Ridgway was given command for its new mission. Ridgway was a West Point graduate who was committed to not squandering his troops and always respected the ordinary soldiers. After a disastrous nocturnal jump over Sicily, Ridgway was ordered to repeat such a jump into the American lines south of the Sele River during the Nazi counter-attack of 13–14 September 1943 that almost evicted the VI Corps from its beachhead. Elements of the 82nd Airborne were to see extensive action in the post-Salerno campaign in a more conventional infantry role. (NARA)

Lieutenant-General Gerard Bucknall is shown in north-west Europe. On 3 September 1943, as a major-general, he led the British 5th Division as part of Montgomery's Eighth Army's XIII Corps in the crossing of the Strait of Messina during Operation Baytown to seize the Reggio di Calabria and begin its arduous northern advance to link up at the Salerno battlefield. As the Italian campaign progressed, Bucknall was to lead his 5th Division as part of Lieutenant-General Allfrey's British V Corps along the Adriatic coast. Bucknall would leave Italy in late December 1943 with his superiors, Montgomery and Dempsey, to begin planning for the Normandy invasion. (NARA)

Major-General John L.T. Hawkesworth (left), commanding general of the British 46th Division, is shown aboard USS Biscayne with US Navy Rear-Admiral Richard L. Conolly (right) on 6 September 1943, as the Allied armada was steaming towards the Gulf of Salerno to launch Operation Avalanche three days later. His division would be on the left of the British X Corps assault just to the east of Salerno and north of the Sele River. On D-Day, Hawkesworth's division beat back attacking waves of the German 16th Panzer Division and then moved towards the town of Salerno under heavy fire. Later in the campaign, at the Garigliano River, the 46th Division failed in its initial attempt to cross the waterway. (NARA)

Shown here with Montgomery in Normandy in June 1944 is Major-General Douglas A.H. Graham, who commanded the British 56th Division, which constituted the right flank of McCreery's X Corps amphibious assault. Graham's division was tasked with the capture of the vital Montecorvino airfield and the high ground to its immediate north as well as seize the railway hub at Battipaglia. (*Author's Collection*)

Brigadier Robert Laycock, commanding officer of the British Special Service Brigade, comprising British Army No. 2 and Royal Marine No. 41 Commandos, is shown reviewing troops. Laycock's force was to land at Vietri and to seize key high ground leading from Salerno to Naples as well as prevent German reinforcements from reaching the Salerno beachhead via Highway 18 or other coastal routes. (*Author's Collection*)

Brigadier-General Robert T. Frederick, commanding officer of the Canadian-American 1st Special Service Force, is shown in early 1944. Previously as a colonel, Frederick led his elite force, which had trained for mountainous warfare in snow-covered terrain, in an unopposed landing at Kiska in the Aleutians in the late summer of 1943. Frederick later arrived in Italy with his unit in November 1943, after Eisenhower ordered them to be utilised in special reconnaissance and raiding operations in Italy's mountainous terrain attached to the US 36th Division of Keyes' II Corps. On the night of 2 December, 1st Special Service Force began their steep ascent to the top of Monte la Difensa, which was reached by dawn on the following day. By the end of 3 December, Frederick's force had taken over a hundred casualties. This unit fought off repeated German counter-attacks to drive them from their positions and, on 5 December, the Germans on Monte la Difensa began to withdraw as British troops secured a neighbouring height, Monte Camino. The 1st Special Service Force had incurred over 500 casualties, including seventy-three members of this elite unit killed in action. Frederick's 1st Special Service Force was to see action again at Monte Sammucro on 24 December, and later during further mountainous combat with the US II Corps. (NARA)

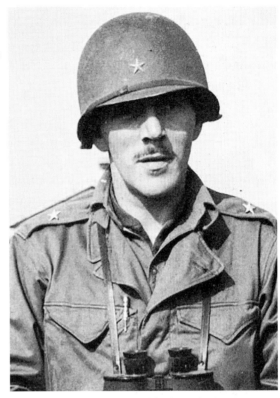

Field Marshal Albert Kesselring, a *Luftwaffe* officer, was appointed commander-in-chief South in December 1941 with his headquarters based near Rome. Prior to that, Kesselring helped create the operational mechanics of the *Luftwaffe*, commanded Hitler's air squadrons in the Mediterranean theatre, and reported to the Italian Fascist leader, Benito Mussolini. Having combat experience in both Poland and France, he was instrumental in the development of tactical aerial assault, notably with his squadrons of Ju 87 or *Stuka* dive bombers in 1939 and 1940, which he brought to the Mediterranean theatre along the North African littoral. During the Sicily Campaign, Kesselring retained tactical authority over all German military units in southern Italy, even though he was a *Luftwaffe* rather than an army officer. At odds with the other German field marshal in Northern Italy, Erwin Rommel, Kesselring advocated for a tenacious defence of southern Italy and the building of defensive fortification belts situated on the peninsula's rugged mountainous terrain and rivers. With Rommel's eventual transfer to Northern France, Hitler acceded to Kesselring's strategy against an Allied invasion of the Italian mainland. Kesselring also wanted to utilise a harsh winter climate, interior lines, and mountain defences as force multipliers. (NARA)

German General Heinrich von Vietinghoff, a First World War veteran, served as commanding general of the Nazi's Tenth Army in southern Italy. Prior to his leadership role in Italy, he was a Panzer division and corps commander in France and Russia, respectively, and served as the German Fifth Army commander in France prior to Operation Husky in July 1943. After the Allied invasion of Sicily, he was dispatched to Italy to assume command of the Tenth Army there, having earned a reputation in Russia as an aggressive armoured commander. Vietinghoff wanted to contest the Salerno landings. In order to accomplish this, he ordered General Hans Hube's XIV Panzer Corps, stationed in the Naples vicinity, to deploy his forces, which had been held in reserve in the event of a landing in the Gulf of Gaeta to the north. (*Author's Collection*)

General Traugott Herr, commanding general of the German LXXVI Panzer Corps, is shown. He was highly successful at disengaging his 29th Panzer Grenadier and 26th Panzer divisions from the British Eighth Army's slow advance and deliver them to the Salerno battlefield, where he was instrumental in orchestrating the Nazi counter-attack of 13 September 1943 that almost compelled Clark to evacuate the US VI Corps from the southern half of the beachhead to the south of the Sele River.

(*Author's Collection*)

General Hans-Valentine Hube, the XIV Panzer Corps commander in Italy, is shown returning to Calabria from Messina after the successful Axis evacuation across the Strait of Messina. Hube had previously commanded the 1st *Panzerarmee* in Russia, serving under Field Marshal Erich von Manstein. The three divisions of the German XIV Panzer Corps had been kept in the general Naples area as the precise landing site of the Allied armada on 9 September was unclear. The 15th Panzer Grenadier Division was stationed at the Gulf of Gaeta, from Terracina in the north to the mouth of the Volturno River. The Hermann Göring Division was situated from the Volturno River to Castellamare on the northern shore of the Sorrento Peninsula. The 16th Panzer Division was to provide an initial stout defence against the Allied landings south of the town of Salerno, as it was situated along the Gulf of Salerno as far south as Agropoli. For the actual combat to repel the Allied invasion, the acting XIV Corps commander was General Hermann Balck, as Hube was on leave. Hube was re-assigned to Russia in November 1943 and his replacement was to be Lieutenant-General Fridolin von Senger und Etterlin. (*NARA*)

Lieutenant-General Fridolin von Senger und Etterlin took over the command of German XIV Corps from Hube in late autumn of 1943 in time for the intense mountain conflicts culminating in the First Battle of Cassino. Intriguingly, Senger und Etterlin had strong roots in Catholicism as well as being a lay Benedictine, which was pertinent since he was to command the defences involved in the Monte Cassino battles. General von Senger und Etterlin was one of Germany's Oxford-educated officers who had decided to fight for their country even though their religious and political views were at odds with Hitler's brutal Nazi regime. A First World War veteran field artilleryman and a post-war Weimar cavalryman, Senger und Etterlin had been a brigade commander during the *Blitzkrieg* in France in the spring of 1940, and led the 17th Panzer Division during the winter campaign of 1942 on the Russian Front. Upon arriving on Sicily in late June 1943, Senger und Etterlin was shocked by the incomplete and disorganised Italian defences of the island's coastline. (*NARA*)

A trio of Canadian infantrymen from New Brunswick's Carleton and York Regiment of the 1st Canadian Division clearing out German snipers in house-to-house fighting in Campochiaro on 23 October 1943, in Central Italy's mountainous region. By early December, as the British 78th Division's drive toward the Moro River Valley on the Adriatic coast was grinding to a halt after suffering more than 4,000 casualties in the crossing of the Sangro River, the 1st Canadian Division was ordered eastward from Campobasso to relieve the 78th. The division's commander, Major-General Guy G. Simonds, who fell ill, was replaced by Major-General Chris Vokes. (NARA)

(**Opposite, above**) A Canadian infantryman serving in the 48th Highlanders of Canada of the 1st Canadian Division in Italy reading signposts in German that were left behind by the withdrawing Nazis after a town on the eastern side of the peninsula was captured. In December 1939, almost 16,000 Canadian soldiers sailed to Britain as part of the 1st Canadian Division. This division, accompanied by the 1st Canadian Army Tank Brigade, landed in Sicily on 10 July 1943 and fought a tenacious Nazi foe. On 3 September, Simonds' 1st Canadian Division landed at Reggio di Calabria as part of the British Eighth Army's XIII Corps. With the Italian surrender and after crossing over to the eastern side of the Apennine Mountains, the Canadians again were to confront stout Nazi divisions in combat. (NARA)

(**Opposite, below**) A 1st Canadian Division platoon leader, Lieutenant Ian Macdonald, of the 48th Highlanders of Canada, is shown holding binoculars (*left background*) to reconnoitre enemy positions prior to resuming the attack near San Leonardo in December 1943. The ensuing battle for Ortona, a coastal town 15 miles north of the Sangro River, was to become a brutal street-fighting conflict as the Germans had turned this locale into a strongpoint. German engineers had purposefully destroyed stone houses to create piles of rubble that blocked streets and impeded the movement of Canadian tanks as well as creating cover for Nazi snipers and tank-destroying *panzerfaust* teams. (NARA)

Paratroopers of a battery of the British 1st Air Landing Light Artillery Regiment attached to the British 5th Division of the newly activated V Corps are shown with their American-made M8 75mm pack Howitzer, which was one of the most powerful weapons that British 1st Airborne had in its armamentarium, when it functioned as light infantry after their assaults were made. This versatile weapon was extremely suitable for infantry support in the mountainous terrain of Italy. Its utility was that it could be stripped down into component parts in seconds for animal packs (thus, the term 'pack' Howitzer) or human transport. On 9 September 1943, the naval base at Taranto was captured by the 1st Airborne Division in an amphibious assault. The paratroopers arrived and found Taranto undefended as the Italian fleet had sailed off after surrendering. However, the harbour was mined. HMS *Abdiel* was sunk after hitting a mine, with a loss of 120 paratroopers and over two scores of Royal Navy seamen. Once ashore, the paratroopers captured the nearby airfield at Grottaglie. Two days later, elements of the British 1st Airborne Division, while patrolling north of the airfield, first met the Germans. The divisional commander, Major-General G.F. Hopkinson, was mortally wounded while visiting one of his units. The paratroopers continued their northerly advance and captured Brindisi, Bari and the airdrome at Foggia, engaging elements of the retreating German 1st Parachute Division along the way. On 16 September, after the crisis at Salerno had passed, patrols of the 1st Canadian Division met elements of the 1st Airborne Division at Metaponto on the Gulf of Taranto as the Eighth Army moved its main strength to the eastern side of the Apennines and the Adriatic coast. *(Author's Collection)*

A Scottish unit in the Eighth Army's British 5th Division is being led through San Onofrio, a southern Italy town near Nicastro to the south of Salerno, by one of its pipers. The advance of the Eighth Army coming up from Calabria had been slowed by a lack of transport and supplies as well as the poor condition of the southern Italian roads, especially those demolished by the retreating Germans. It has been speculated that a more rapid arrival of the Eighth Army on the German flank at Salerno would have made a difference in the battle waged there. *(NARA)*

(**Opposite, above**) A British X Corps Bren-gun team taking cover on the floor of a deserted farmhouse on the outskirts of the town of Salerno, which was assaulted by the British 46th Division with nearby elements of Laycock's 2nd Special Service Brigade's Commandos. (*NARA*)

(**Above**) A British X Corps Universal carrier entering an Italian town north of Salerno, with a signpost for 'Napoli', indicating the direction to the next destination, Naples. This carrier was being utilised as a mobile 3in mortar platform with a spare round and ammunition tubes visible. This weapon was highly favoured for infantry support as it weighed just over 120lb and fired high explosive, smoke and illuminating rounds. After a longer barrel was configured in 1942, the range of this mortar increased to over 2,700 yards. (*NARA*)

(**Opposite, below**) To the north of Salerno, British X Corps infantrymen are shown scaling a stone wall with fixed bayonets in an Italian town in pursuit of the enemy after the failed Nazi counter-attack of mid-September 1943 on their approach to Naples. McCreery's X Corps, upon exiting from Naples, advanced towards the Volturno River, which they would reach by 5 October via Highways 6 and 7 as well as coastal roads. At the river's southern bank, the British met strong resistance from the Nazi 15th Panzer Grenadier and Hermann Göring divisions on the northern side of the waterway, between Capua and Castel Volturno on the coast of the Tyrrhenian Sea. (*NARA*)

(**Above**) British soldiers from the 6th Battalion, Queens Regiment of X Corps' 169th Infantry Brigade of the 56th Division are shown running past two damaged Panzer IV enemy tanks after the failed Nazi counter-attack of mid-September 1943 against the beachhead. In addition to the effectiveness of Allied M4 medium tanks and naval gunfire, the use of the excellent British 6-pounder anti-tank (AT) gun proved vital in stopping the German armoured counter-offensive in mid-September against the X Corps sector. (*NARA*)

(**Opposite, above**) A British infantry section takes cover behind a stone wall along the bank of a tributary of the Sarno River at Scarfati during the X Corps advance towards Naples. At the end of September 1943, McCreery directed the 7th Armoured Division and attached infantry to drive west and secure bridgeheads across the Sarno River. However, the Naples Plain was covered with thickly wooded fruit orchards and narrow-laned villages, like the one showed above, which interfered with the adequate deployment of the tanks and vision of the tankers. (*NARA*)

(**Opposite, below**) British infantrymen of the 56th Division's 1st London Scottish Regiment, in winter coats, clearing a stone farmhouse in the village of Colle in the Monte Camino sector in early December 1943. After initially failing to take Monte Camino in early November, renewed efforts of the X Corps divisions finally captured the height on 10 December, after brutal and protracted combat against the German 15th Panzer Grenadier Division. Due to the masonry structure of buildings like the farmhouse shown above, the enemy often turned them into fortified positions that had to be cleared one at a time. (*NARA*)

American paratroopers of the 504th Parachute Infantry Regiment (PIR) of the US 82nd Airborne, attached to Major-General Lucas's VI Corps, are shown fighting as conventional infantry as they man a 0.30-inch calibre machine-gun in the doorway of a destroyed house north of Isernia in mid-December. Clark's Fifth Army was slowly advancing through horrible terrain as winter weather set in. (NARA)

(**Opposite, above**) A unit of US Rangers manning a firing line in the Castellamare sector on the northern tip of the Sorrento Peninsula. Three battalions under Lieutenant William O. Darby, including many veterans of North Africa and Sicily, initially landed on 9 September 1943 at Maiori to the south-west of the town of Salerno. After seizing and holding the vital Chiunzi Pass 5 miles inland overlooking the Naples Plain from ten days of repeated Nazi counter-attacks, the 1st and 3rd Ranger battalions marched approximately 10 miles to Castellammare on 29 September and bivouaced near the seaside town on the Gulf of Gaeta later to be joined by the 4th Battalion. (NARA)

(**Opposite, below**) Canadian soldiers of Colonel (later Brigadier-General) Robert Frederick's 1st Special Service Force (SSF) are shown getting a last-minute briefing before a mission in front of an Italian farm's haystack. The 1st SSF comprised three regiments with two battalions, each commanded by a lieutenant-colonel. The 1st SSF in its combat debut had spearheaded an amphibious landing on Kiska in the Aleutian Islands against the Japanese, who had deserted the island three days before the Allied force arrived. In November 1943, Clark needed an elite unit to capture Monte la Difensa, which was the key to the Mignano Gap. Having had rigorous mountain and snow-covered terrain training, Frederick's force began their assault on Monte la Difensa in the early hours of 3 December. They would combat the Nazi defenders on the mountaintop and nearby height, during Operation Raincoat, for the next few days. After being pulled out of the line for eleven days, the 1st SSF was to see subsequent action at Montes Maio and Vischiataro. (NARA)

(**Above**) A patrol of the US 45th Infantry Division, led by a soldier of Native American descent, is shown marching along a hillside trail after the Salerno conflict ended in late September 1943. The Thunderbirds, veterans of Sicily, were men of a national guard division from Oklahoma, Arizona, Colorado and New Mexico. According to historian Flint Whitlock, the division's roots 'go back to the settling of the Wild West; the early antecedents of which saw service in the Civil War, the Spanish-American War, and the Punitive Expedition against Pancho Villa, as well as World War I'. Thousands of Native Americans were incorporated into the division's ranks. (*NARA*)

(**Opposite, above**) A US 45th Infantry Division soldier, Private Tallbird, a Cheyenne Indian, is shown amusing a British Bren-gun team with his drawings of Indian chiefs. Native-Americans within the 45th Division contributed to the heroic action at Salerno. (*NARA*)

(**Opposite, below**) Private Arthur Shinyama of the US 442nd Infantry Regiment of the 34th Division is shown firing his Browning Automatic Rifle at the enemy from a concealing thicket in 1944. This regiment comprised all Japanese-Americans, or *Nisei*. It became one of the most highly decorated units of the US Army during the war. (*NARA*)

Soldiers of the Japanese-American or *Nisei* 442nd Infantry Regiment of the 34th Division are shown congregating to open mail and gift parcels from stateside. Many German soldiers were astonished to meet 'Japanese' soldiers as an enemy on the Italian battlefield. *(NARA)*

African American fighter pilots of the US Fifteenth Air Force receiving a briefing before a mission in Italy. Pilots from this 99th Fighter Squadron were to claim dozens of *Luftwaffe* kills over the Italian battlefields. *(NARA)*

Lieutenant-General Lucian Truscott reviewing troops of the all-African-American 92nd Buffalo Division in the US Fifth Army. This unit was to go on to be awarded three Legions of Merit and thirteen Silver Stars for gallantry in action. (NARA)

Two New Zealanders of the 2nd New Zealand Division guarding a group of German paratroopers near an Allied M4 medium tank outside the town of Cassino, along a rocky hillside trail by the Rapido River in early 1944. The unique helmets and long parachutist smocks were characteristic uniform components of this elite German combat arm. (*NARA*)

A New Zealand infantryman of the Maori 28th Battalion guarding a group of German prisoners behind a stone wall for protection from Allied artillery fire during the First Battle of Cassino in early 1944. On 3 February, two divisions of the Eighth Army, the 2nd New Zealand and the 4th Indian, were formed into the New Zealand Corps under Freyberg and re-deployed from the moribund Adriatic Front to relieve the shattered American 34th Division of US II Corps exhausted from their quest to capture Cassino. *(NARA)*

Sappers from the 6th South African Armoured Division are shown stacking German landmines in early 1944. South African troops had fought gallantly in the Middle East and this armoured unit was to serve as part of both the Fifth and Eighth armies. (NARA)

A trio of Basuto Pioneers, comprising volunteers from the South African tribe, erecting a sapling road for some bogged-down M4 medium tanks along the Sangro River Front in December 1943. The government of South Africa, due to its race policies, did not arm its tribesmen. Instead, a native military corps was formed to be manned by black South Africans for pioneer, motor, labour and guard duties. (NARA)

An 8th Indian Division Punjabi Regiment patrol reconnoiters enemy positions as part of V Corps along the Adriatic Sea Front to the east of the Apennine Mountains. In the autumn of 1943, V Corps was formed with the 8th Indian, British 78th and elements of the British 1st Airborne divisions. The 8th Indian Division's advance was met with sharp combat from the German LXXVI Corps' 16th and 26th Panzer, 29th Panzer Grenadier and 1st Parachute divisions across the Biferno, Trigno and Sangro rivers. Later on, the advance of the 8th Indian Division converged with the 1st Canadian Division, towards Ortona north of the Moro River. (*USAMHI*)

(**Above**) A Canadian soldier admiring the *kukri* fighting knife proudly displayed by two Gurkhas of the 8th Indian Regiment in British V Corps along the Adriatic coast sector as part of the Eighth Army's sustained offensive towards Ortona in December 1943. *(NARA)*

(**Opposite**) A Jewish Independent Brigade gunner preparing to load his 25-pounder gun with a shell with Hebrew writing and a Star of David emblem. Jews from the Palestine Mandate fought in the Eighth Army across North Africa. During the Italian Campaign, there was one independent brigade within the Eighth Army participating in the combat. *(NARA)*

(**Above**) Polish soldiers are shown carrying a dead comrade from the war-ravaged terrain of Monte Cassino. To the left of the Polish infantrymen were dead German defenders of the town and monastery. The over two-year odyssey of these Polish soldiers who fought in the Allied Fifth Army spanned three continents. Their trek started from Soviet captivity to the east of Moscow into the south-eastern Central Asian republics. From there, the Poles continued their travels through Persia into the British-controlled Middle East, where they were to be designated as Polish II Corps under General Wladyslaw Anders. Ultimately re-equipped and recuperated from their ordeal, they departed from Egypt for Italy's Adriatic coast and then to the battlefields at Cassino. (*NARA*)

(**Opposite**) French Expeditionary Corps (FEC) soldiers of the 3rd Squadron, 3rd Regiment di Spahis, 2nd Moroccan Division are shown manning their American .30-inch calibre American-made Browning light machine-gun during their late January 1944 offensive across the Rapido River north of Cassino, after the failed II Corps attack by the US 36th Division further to the south. The 2nd Moroccan Division crossed the Rapido successfully on 24 January. The FEC was composed of more than 100,000 troops and consisted of 60 per cent North African and 40 per cent French, the latter mainly émigrés from Metropolitan France who resided in Algiers, Oran and Constantine. (*NARA*)

(**Above**) Gunners of a French Expeditionary Corps (FEC) 105mm Howitzer battery firing their artillery piece in support of the 3rd Algerian Division, which successfully crossed the Rapido Rive at Sant' Elia in late January 1944. The gunners are shown wearing the classic Adrian steel helmet of the French Army, which was devised in 1915 as the M15 helmet. A subsequent version, the M26, was used by French forces during the Second World War. The Algerians took Monte Belvedere and Colle Abate, but due to a lack of reinforcements were unable to hold the latter position and had to halt its advance. (*NARA*)

(**Opposite, above**) Moroccan Goumiers manning an American 0.30-inch calibre Browning light machine-gun in the rubble of an Italian village north of Cassino on the French Expeditionary Corps (FEC) Front in January 1944. The machine-gun-crewmen are wearing their characteristic woollen striped *djellbah*, or long coats, of the mountain tribesmen from North Africa along with British War Office-patterned Mk I 'Brodie'-style steel helmets, which refers to the design in 1915 by John Leopold Brodie. (*NARA*)

(**Opposite, below**) Berber mounted horsemen from the 2nd Goum of the 2nd Moroccan Division on their Arabian steeds setting out for a reconnaissance patrol in the foothills of the inhospitable Aurunci Mountains after French Expeditionary Corps (FEC) commander Juin's troops were re-deployed to the Garigliano River sector. The Germans believed that the Aurunci Mountains terrain would protect their flanks. However, the lightly burdened Moroccan Goumiers captured Monte Maio, which threatened the Nazi right flank in the Liri Valley. They are wearing their customary native garb and were equipped with both British and American gear. To the enemy they were known for both their ruthlessness and ability to traverse harsh terrain. (*NARA*)

Two Italians soldiers, who have left their disbanded unit after the armistice was signed between the Italian government and the Allies on 8 September 1943, marching past a disabled German Flak 88 anti-aircraft (AA) gun and its towing vehicle near Taranto. Fortunately for the British 1st Airborne Division, their amphibious assault on Taranto on 9 September was uncontested. This was unlike the situation on the Tyrrhenian coast on that same day, where these excellent guns were effectively used as artillery pieces by gunners of the German 16th Panzer Division, to score several hits on British landing craft in the opening phases of Operation Avalanche on the beaches just south of the town of Salerno. The gun did have a very high silhouette, which made it vulnerable to high explosive offshore naval gunfire supporting the amphibious landings. (*NARA*)

Italian troops of the 2nd Battalion, 68th Infantry Regiment, who were now Allies, are shown having their weapons inspected by American infantrymen in mid-December 1943. The 1st Italian Motorised Group came under the control of the Allied 15th Army Group on 31 October 1943. However, it was well below Allied standards in training, weapons and equipment at its inception. After intensive training, this 5,500-man regiment was moved into bivouac near Capua on 22 November. Early in December, it was attached to the US II Corps and committed into action in the Mignano area. An attack made by 1,600 Italians from this unit on Monte Lungo on 7 December in support of the US 141st Infantry Regiment of the 36th Division failed to evict the Germans from their positions while having incurred several hundred casualties. (*NARA*)

A German artillery battery situated along a tree-lined road during the Allied advance from the hard-won Salerno beachhead towards Naples in late September 1943. On 20 September, US VI Corps, under their new commander Major-General John Lucas, moved out from the right flank of the beachhead with the intention of carrying out an envelopment to the north-west, outflanking Naples and reaching the Volturno River to the east of Capua. Field Marshal Kesselring had instructed his troops to withdraw from the Salerno area in an orderly fashion and to delay the Allied advance as to allow General von Vietinghoff to hold the Volturno River Line until 15 October. On 23 September, McCreery's X Corps moved out to take the two passes through the hills north of Salerno, the Chiunzi and Molina Passes. However, little progress was made due to German rearguard activity and autumn rain. Clark reinforced Darby's Rangers with the US 82nd Airborne at these locales, and the combined force attached to X Corps made it through the mountain passes onto the Naples Plain. These units were to enter Naples on 1 October. Some 50 miles to the north of Naples, Kesselring had fortified a line through Mignano, the Bernhardt Line, for a strong defence in the Italian mountains as colder November weather was to set in north of the Volturno River. *(NARA)*

A German machine-gunner with his still-loaded weapon is shown lying dead in his dugout position amid the rubble of Ortona, 15 miles north of the Sangro River. During that seven-day epic battle of street-fighting, the combat tenacity among the Nazi infantrymen and parachutists was always displayed. *(NARA)*

Chapter Four

Operations Baytown, Slapstick and Avalanche at Reggio Calabria, Taranto and Salerno

Operation Baytown, the crossing of the Strait of Messina to the toe of Italy at Reggio di Calabria, commenced at 0430hrs on 3 September 1943. British XIII Corps of Montgomery's Eighth Army had tremendous air, naval and artillery support for the first large-scale Allied invasion of continental Europe. British Army Commandos accompanied the amphibious landings, which were uncontested by the Axis forces, just days before Italy's capitulation. Two Nazi divisions, the 29th Panzer Grenadier and 26th Panzer, began to withdraw after starting their pattern of extensive demolitions of infrastructure. Without adequate motor transport, British XIII Corps' northward advance was slow.

On 8 September 1943, a small amphibious attack involving the 231st Independent Brigade under Brigadier Robert 'Roy' Urquhart, transpired at Pizzo, about 50 miles from Reggio. After some initial combat with a 26th Panzer Division *kampfgruppe*, the Nazis chose to withdraw northward in an orderly fashion. The absence of a larger scale enemy response was due, in part, to the spotting of Allied ships on their course towards the Gulf of Salerno.

Operation Slapstick involved 3,600 airborne troops of the 1st British Airborne Division, entering Taranto Harbour on 9 September 1943, sailing in light cruisers and minelayers preceded by minesweepers. No German forces were there, and Italian troops manning the defences, who had just surrendered to the Allies, welcomed the British paratroopers. A British minelaying cruiser, HMS *Abdiel*, sank after striking a mine in the harbour, with heavy casualties incurred. Nonetheless, the port of Taranto was in excellent condition. After the Italian surrender on 8 September, the Italian Navy turned over major elements of their fleet to the Allies at Taranto. After the port-city's occupation, British paratroopers moved off in search of the enemy on 11 September and, following some encounters with the German 1st Parachute

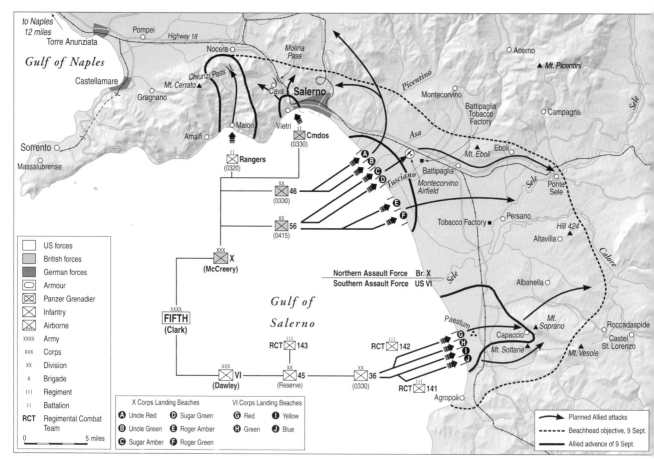

Operation Avalanche, the Allied invasion of the Italian mainland at Salerno, 9 September 1943.
General Clark's Fifth Army divided into a British X Corps (Northern Assault Force under Lieutenant-General McCreery) and a US VI Corps (Southern Assault Force under Major-General Dawley) assaulted the Gulf of Salerno beaches early on 9 September. US Army Rangers and British Commandos landed at Maiori and Vietri to seize and hold the Chiunzi and Molina Passes, near Nocera and Cava, respectively, to prevent German troop movement towards the beaches from Naples and further north via Highway 18. Both the British 46th and 56th divisions landed north of the Sele River on D-Day, with the former on the left at Uncle sector's Red and Green beaches. Separate 46th Division columns moved to take Salerno through the Picentino valley. To the south of the Asa River, elements of the 56th Division landed at Sugar Amber beach. The rest of the 56th Division landed at Sugar Green and the Roger sector beaches, designated Amber and Green, with the Montecorvino Airfield and railway hub at Battipaglia as objectives. US VI Corps landed south of the Sele River at Paestum at four beaches designated as Red, Green, Yellow and Blue. Red Beach was 8 miles from the southernmost British landing area, with the Sele River effectively splitting the Fifth Army into two separate fronts. Behind Paestum, two mountains, Mt Soprano at 3,556 feet and Mt Sottane at 2,978 feet, dominated the battlefield. US VI Corps landings were made by the 36th division's 141st and 142nd regimental combat teams (RCTs) with that division's 143rd RCT and two RCTs of the US 45th Division held as floating reserve. The VI Corps assault plan called for advances onto Altavilla and Hill 424, establishing the Fifth Army's right flank for an eventual link-up with forward units of the British X Corps near Ponte Sele. *(Philip Schwartzberg, Meridian Mapping, Minneapolis, MN)*

Division, the British Red Devils occupied Brindisi on the Adriatic coast without opposition. Elements of the German 1st Parachute Division withdrew toward Foggia with its important airdrome there, and maintained light contact and delaying tactics on the pursuing British.

The invasion armada for Operation Avalanche, the Allied invasion in the Gulf of Salerno, commenced sailing during the first week of September 1943, with British X Corps having embarked from Tripoli and Bizerte. Dawley's US VI Corps assault division, the 36th, sailed from Oran, while the floating reserve division, the 45th, disembarked from Palermo. Overall command of the armada was under Vice Admiral H. Kent Hewitt, who had been involved in the earlier north-west African and Sicilian invasions. German reconnaissance aircraft had spotted the armada but were uncertain about its destination. Kesselring did not have the available troops to defend all possible sites of Allied amphibious assaults.

The separate Allied convoys comprising the Northern (British X Corps) and Southern Attack (US VI Corps) forces arrived off of the invasion beaches in the Gulf of Salerno at 2200hrs on 8 September; just hours after Eisenhower announced the Italian government's capitulation to the Allies. Although there was no longer any Italian resistance to the invasion, the new Nazi occupiers of Italy were to combat the assault waves with ferocity. The Northern Attack Force opted for a preliminary naval bombardment, as they had already been sighted. However, the Southern Attack Force with US VI Corps, decided not to fire a preparatory naval bombardment so they could maintain surprise. To overcome the limited Allied naval air umbrella, the Montecorvino airfield ashore to the east of the town of Salerno in British X Corps sector became of prime import to seize for land-based Allied fighters.

In the original planning, Dawley's US VI Corps' 36th and 45th divisions were to land to the south of the Sele between Paestum and the river and occupy ground above the Salerno Plain from its eastern and southern sides. However, due to a shortage of landing craft, only two RCTs from the US 36th Division, a Texas National Guard unit, made the initial assault. Two RCTs from the US 45th Division and the 36th's third RCT were held as the Fifth Army's floating reserve. A planned link-up between the two Allied corps was to occur at Ponte Sele to the east of Eboli and north of Altavilla, the latter where the Calore River, a tributary of the Sele, flows around to the north and then the west. The US 3rd and 34th Infantry divisions, along with the 1st US Armoured Division, were scheduled to come ashore through Naples once the port was occupied by the Allies. The US 82nd Airborne Division was held in reserve at airfields on Sicily, but was to be urgently employed within days of the invasion.

Kesselring and Vietinghoff realised that Montgomery's invasion at Reggio di Calabria and the British 1st Airborne Division's amphibious assault at Taranto did not constitute the major Allied effort, nor were they major threats. Despite the Allied armada being spotted by enemy reconnaissance aircraft, three US Ranger battalions met no immediate resistance at their landing area near Maiori at 0320hrs, and advanced east towards the town of Salerno and west along the northern shores of the Gulf of Salerno towards Amalfi near the southern base of the Sorrento Peninsula. Other ranger units seized one of the main objectives, the Chiunzi Pass at the top of a mountain, which was part of the range that ringed the narrow beach strip within the entire Gulf of Salerno. British Army and Royal Marine Commandos of the 2nd Special Service Brigade initially arrived uncontested at 0330hrs at Vietri, a small fishing port. However, a sharp firefight ensued. Despite the encounter, Laycock's Commando units were able to maintain possession of the small port and move east to assist with the occupation of the town of Salerno.

Leaving a gap of several miles to the Commandos' right, the British 46th Division landed, under a heavy naval bombardment, just to the south of the town of Salerno and, despite meeting German resistance, these troops moved directly inland toward the Montecorvino airfield between the Asa and Tusciano rivers, and north-west towards the town of Salerno. Brigades from the British 56th Division, landing on the beaches opposite the rail centre of Battipaglia, encountered some Nazi armour, which was sent fleeing by Allied naval gunfire. Initial movements into Battipaglia by the British 56th Division occurred, but attempts to seize the nearby high ground in order to secure the Montecorvino airfield faltered.

The 36th Division landed south of the Sele River near the ancient Greek town of Paestum. A gap of approximately 7 miles separated the two Allied corps, with the Sele River running through it. The 36th Division's assault with two RCTs abreast of one another, the 141st and 142nd, was without naval bombardment. However, the Germans responded with artillery gunfire and chaos began to reign on the beaches and among offshore Allied vessels, with heavy casualties being taken by the first of six waves of assaulting American infantrymen. With grit and fortitude, the US 36th Division infantrymen moved inland to the railroad that paralleled their assault beaches, reaching this site in the late afternoon with plans to move north-eastward towards Altavilla in the vicinity of Hill 424.

The separate Allied beachheads on D-Day offered inviting targets for a German response. Out of direct telephone or radio communication with Field Marshal Kesselring, Vietinghoff had decided on D-Day that he would repel the invasion at Salerno with the 16th Panzer Division that had been situated in the Salerno vicinity. This Panzer division was the only fully equipped Nazi armoured unit in southern Italy. This Nazi formation had constructed eight strongpoints near the shoreline between Salerno and Agropoli. The 16th Panzer Division's initial fifteen-tank assault was driven back by US naval, artillery and infantry gunfire. Other elements of this Panzer division, spread over a wide area, fought alone and took the full force of the invasion. With its dispersion, the 16th Panzer Division on 9 September 1943 launched only small concentrated tank-infantry counter-attacks rather than a massed armoured response. By the end of D-Day, only thirty-five 16th Panzer Division tanks were operational. However, these limited Nazi counter-attacks near the shoreline had inflicted hundreds of casualties on the Allied assaulting infantry.

General Vietinghoff was confronted as to how to reinforce the solitary 16th Panzer Division. To Salerno's north, the 15th Panzer Grenadier and Hermann Göring divisions of the XIV Panzer Corps, were only partially reconstituted after combat on Sicily and evacuation to Italy in mid-August 1943. Allied aerial reconnaissance had observed that the main elements of German 29th Panzer Grenadier and 26th Panzer divisions from the LXXVI Panzer Corps, although withdrawing north from Calabria since 3 September, were still remote from the Gulf of Salerno beaches to contest the Allied D-Day landings. However, sufficient elements of the German 29th Panzer Grenadier Division were present to thwart the US 36th Division's move on Altavilla.

Later on D-Day, Clark sent ashore the 36th Division's remaining RCT to bolster the American lines that were consolidating its beachhead. Early on 10 September, the 45th Division's 179th RCT came ashore and moved into an assembly area along the coastal highway north of Paestum to pass from the Fifth Army reserve to VI Corps control. The 157th RCT of the 45th Division also disembarked from the floating reserve into the US VI Corps beachhead later on D-Day +1.

Kesselring shifted regimental-sized elements of the 3rd Panzer Grenadier Division from the vicinity of Rome to a more proximate locale in the vicinity of the Gulf of Gaeta. The German field marshal remained apprehensive about other Allied amphibious operations that might occur to Salerno's north.

Although the Germans were still not concentrated, Nazi resistance against British X Corps stiffened on 11 September 1943. US VI Corps moved two RCTs of the US 45th Division and a regiment of the 36th Division to close the gap between the British and American forces. Dawley's extensive VI Corps frontage was being manned by an increasingly attenuated American combat force erecting a defensive line facing south-east to protect the beachhead against the remainder of the LXXVI Panzer Corps' troops that were arriving from Calabria.

Also, on 11 September, British troops finally captured the Montecorvino airfield, but it could not service Allied fighters as it was under German artillery fire. However, some of the Royal Navy's Seafire fighters were dispatched to a strip near Paestum to become the first land-based fighters at Salerno. Over 500 *Luftwaffe* sorties were flown primarily against the landing armada, which sank four transports, a heavy cruiser and some landing craft. The Nazis also implemented their new radio-controlled guided bombs to attack Allied shipping, which were to subsequently damage two Allied cruisers and two hospital ships.

On the night of 11–12 September, battalion-sized elements of the 15th Panzer Grenadier Regiment of the 29th Panzer Grenadier Division began to infiltrate around

Hill 424 in the vicinity of Altavilla, and bitter fighting ensued against the companies of the 36th Division's 142nd Infantry Regiment, eventually severing the lines between the American infantry battalions. A larger US force would be needed to retake and hold Altavilla from the Nazi defenders.

Elsewhere in the American sector on 11 September, the Germans had drove the 45th Division's 179th Infantry Regiment from the river bluffs overlooking Ponte Sele, but the Nazis were exposed to an attack in the vicinity of Persano by that division's 157th Regiment west of the Sele River. During the night of 11–12 September, the Germans withdrew from Persano. At daybreak on 12 September, elements of the 45th Division's 179th Infantry Regiment, accompanied by a company from the 753rd Tank Battalion, occupied Persano and prepared to more firmly establish its contact with its 157th Infantry Regiment.

On 12 September, Companies A and B from the 45th Division's 157th Infantry Regiment continued its attack on the Tobacco Factory, but the German defenders were steadfast with their AT and machine-gunfire. After battling for over an hour, the Nazis withdrew northwards towards Eboli and this locale was in American hands before noon. However, typical German counter-attacks followed, which drove the American infantrymen out of the Tobacco Factory, only for US artillery and tank fire to enable a battalion from the 157th Infantry to reclaim the site north-west of Persano by the onset of dusk.

Other elements of the German LXXVI Panzer Corps were also in northward transit. British Eighth Army's advance had been tedious, which enabled German counter-attacks on the Fifth Army's beachhead to be mounted without mutual support from Montogomery's forces. By 12 September, fresh elements of the 26th Panzer Division and the 29th Panzer Grenadier Division had reinforced the 16th Panzer Division in the area between Battipaglia and Eboli. From the north, the Hermann Göring Division, along with elements of the 15th Panzer Grenadier Division, had formed a striking force in the vicinity of the Molina Pass to prepare a counter-attack against the British X Corps. The 3rd Panzer Grenadier Division had fielded a battalion to the north-east of the town of Salerno.

On the night of 12 September, units of the German 29th Panzer Grenadier Division, spearheaded by over a score of tanks, attacked between the flanks of Clark's Fifth Army, where almost a 5-mile gap between US and British units near the Sele River to the south of Battipaglia existed. The Nazi armoured counter-attack drove the 167th Brigade of the British 56th Division out of Battipaglia with heavy Allied losses. The British were unable to recapture Battipaglia, despite the presence of the 56th Division's 201st Guards Brigade. The German capture of Battipaglia made further reinforcement of the Fifth Army's left flank imperative.

After almost four days of scattered engagements throughout the shallow beach-head, Vietinghoff, on 13 September, sensing the precarious state of the VI Corps defences as Dawley continued to shift his forces, launched an extensive counter-attack stretching from the Vietri Pass in the north to Altavilla in the south. The German aim was to drive through the British X and US VI Corps' gap in the Sele River corridor. Multiple major axes of Nazi counter-attacks were unleashed on 13 September. In the north, units from the Hermann Göring and 15th Panzer Grenadier divisions attacked the British X Corps sector from the north of Vietri. From between Battipaglia and Eboli, elements of the German 16th Panzer Division attacked the Tobacco Factory and also southwards past Persano in the area marking the confluence of the Sele and Calore rivers. At the Tobacco Factory, attacks and counter-attacks by both sides with greater force and persistence occurred on 13 September pitting elements of the 1st Battalion, US 157th Infantry Regiments against Nazi tanks and a battalion-sized infantry force of the German 79th Panzer Grenadier Regiment of the 16th Panzer Division. Over 500 men from the 2nd Battalion, 143rd US Infantry Regiment were lost in the hectic tank-infantry combat in the Sele-Calore corridor, delivered by elements of the German 29th Panzer Grenadier Division. To the southeast, elements of the 15th Panzer Grenadier Regiment of the 29th Panzer Grenadier Division, swept over both sides of Hill 424 and converged on Altavilla.

As 13 September, or 'Black Monday', wore on, German troops converged on the junction of the Sele and Calore rivers against the precariously thin line of Americans, and penetrated the US VI Corps lines, overrunning a battalion of the 36th Division and threatening the rear of the Allied position. Walker's 36th Division drew troops from every possible source, including American support troops and artillerymen. Tank and tank destroyer crews fired rounds point blank along the Calore River within a perimeter 5 miles from the shoreline that staunched the Nazi armoured thrust that tried to drive the Americans into the sea. By nightfall of that critical day, the German attacks had ebbed and the Allied lines started to become reconstituted. Allied commanders realised that the American VI Corps troops had been over-extended.

On 13 September 1943, the Eighth Army was still more than 100 miles from Salerno. Montgomery was exhorted by Alexander to make contact with northerly withdrawing Germans to delay any additional Nazi formations from mounting attacks against the Fifth Army beachhead. Clark's Fifth Army headquarters near Paestum was transferred from the US VI Corps sector to the less-threatened British X Corps zone. Plans were even discussed by Clark to evacuate the beachhead, if needed, which rankled some British senior naval and army commanders who, perhaps, remembered similar ignoble seaborne withdrawals at Dunkirk, Greece and Crete. In the end, American infantry withdrew to a new defence line 2 miles closer to the shore and hastily erected defensive fortifications to fight rather than evacuate. Vietinghoff had been confident that the Allies would be thrown into the sea at Salerno. However, the high-water-mark of the German counter-attack never advanced past the confluence of the Calore and Sele rivers between Eboli and Altavilla.

The Allied High Command hastily moved air, naval and infantry assets to the Salerno battlefield. Clark, in a desperate move after the recent airborne disasters over Sicily, ordered Ridgway's US 82nd Airborne Division to make a night-time parachute drop into Fifth Army lines on 13 September. Before midnight, 1,300 paratroopers of the 1st and 2nd Battalions of the 504th PIR jumped into the Allied beachhead near Paestum, with rigid AA fire control from offshore Allied shipping to prevent a repeat of the tragic downing of Allied transports over Sicily two months earlier. After a successful parachute drop into the perimeter, the men of the 82nd were then trucked to final defensive positions north of Monte Soprano and west of Albanella.

On 14 September 1943, units of the German 26th Panzer Division, having arrived from Calabria, concentrated for an attack on the town of Salerno against the British 46th Division, which was also bracing itself for a Nazi assault north of Vietri. As the 46th Division held on along their defensive line, the Germans shifted their armoured attack from Battipaglia to an open plain area to the south-east defended by the British 56th Division. The German assault did not penetrate the 56th Division's lines as the Coldstream Guards and Royal Fusiliers held their ground. The British 7th Armoured Division was to arrive soon that day in the X Corps sector. By the evening of 14 September, the gap between the left and right flanks of the Fifth Army south-east of Battipaglia continued to close.

Along the southern sector, the German 29th Panzer Grenadier and 16th Panzer divisions also attacked on 14 September to the south of Eboli and Altavilla against US VI Corps lines. Nazi thrusts continued north of the Sele in the US 45th Division sector near the Tobacco Factory as well as in the US 36th Division area in the Sele-Calore river corridor. By the end of the day, the American lines had held after a loss of more than thirty Nazi tanks. The US VI Corps lines remained where they had been reconstituted at dawn on 14 September. The Nazi counter-attacks of 12 and 13 September had forced VI Corps forces out of Altavilla, the Sele-Calore corridor and the Tobacco Factory, and had partly achieved Vietinghoff's intent to attempt a breakthrough towards VI Corps beaches and thwart the American advances toward an area between Eboli and Ponte Sele. At the end of 14 September, the Nazis were unable to exploit their gains from the two previous days. Half of the German armoured strength to contest the Salerno invasion was lost from 9–14 September

The American infantry had been assisted by naval gunfire targeting the Battipaglia-Eboli Road as well as from US medium and heavy bomber sorties. At this time, Clark no longer had any plans to evacuate the Salerno beachhead as he reinforced the VI Corps sector. The third RCT of US 45th Division, the 180th, had landed early on 14 September and was in reserve near Monte Soprano. An additional 2,100 paratroopers of the 505th PIR, 82nd Airborne Division made another nocturnal drop into the American lines during the night of 14–15 September. The 325th Glider regimental combat team disembarked from LCIs on 15 September. Also, the

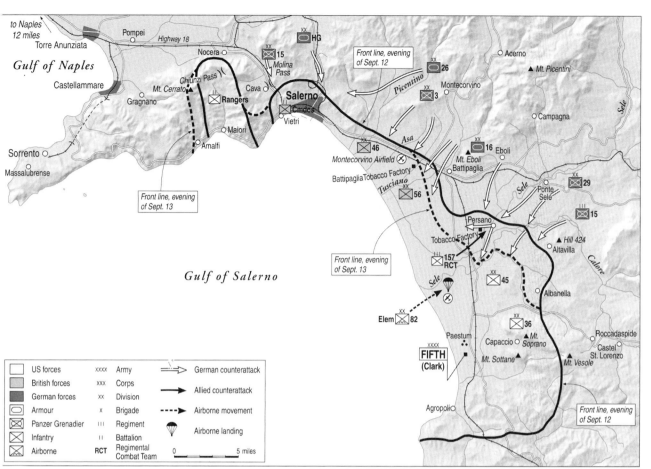

Fifth Army front lines on 12–13 September 1943 and the German counter-attack. The extensive German Tenth Army counter-attacks all along the Allied frontage, on 13 September (Black Monday) by major elements of at least six Panzer and *panzergrenadier* divisions, wreaked havoc against the Fifth Army lines with dire conditions, especially in the US VI Corps sector. The 504th Parachute Infantry Regiment (PIR) of the US 82nd Airborne Division made a daring evening parachute drop into the US VI Corps zone on 13 September, with the veteran American paratrooper battalions rushed to bolster the frontlines prior to a renewed Nazi assault on 14 September. Further American reinforcements, another PIR of the 82nd Airborne Division, and the 180th regimental combat team (RCT) of the US 45th Division arrived near Paestum on the evening of 14 September. Brutal fighting was to continue until 19 September, when the German Tenth Army began its orderly withdrawal from the Gulf of Salerno battlefields. (*Philip Schwartzberg, Meridian Mapping, Minneapolis, MN*)

2nd Battalion, 509th PIR, 82nd Airborne Division was dropped near Avellino, 20 miles to the north of Salerno, to assist the British X Corps with Nazi counter-attacks staged from the mountains north of Maiori and Vietri. However, Allied transports dropped their paratroopers miles from their intended landing zone. Only fifteen of the forty air transports placed their paratroopers within 4 miles of designated target. After several days of conducting only small raids on German supply areas that were supporting enemy attacks on the British X Corps Front, about 400 of the 2nd Battalion's men of the 509th PIR eventually made it back to Fifth Army lines at Salerno.

On 15 September, with the Eighth Army still 50 miles to the south, Kesselring ordered a final large-scale attack against the Salerno beachhead, which failed. Subsequent attacks on 16 September indicated to the German field marshal that the Fifth Army beachhead would remain intact. Only small-scale German attacks ensued, and by 17 September, Kesselring approved Vietinghoff's plans to abandon Battipaglia and withdraw in an orderly manner towards the hastily constructed line of fortifications along the Volturno River, 25 miles north of Naples. Vietinghoff's Tenth Army had delayed the Allied entry into Naples, enabling the Germans to destroy much of the city and the port.

On 18 September, as the Germans withdrew, British tanks and infantry from the 56th Division entered Battipaglia while American forces moved on Ponte Sele. Many of the Fifth Army's beleaguered units had to first consolidate their positions before resuming their advance to Naples. Additionally, through to 1 October, the remainder of the British 7th Armoured, the US 3rd Infantry, and the remainder of the US 82nd Airborne divisions were to come ashore through Salerno to join the Fifth Army for the northward advance. On 19 September, elements of the British 56th Division secured the Montecorvino airfield from Nazi artillery fire and the US 45th Division entered Eboli. By 19 September, elements of the Eighth Army met forward units of the Fifth Army at Auletta, 20 miles east of Eboli.

(**Opposite, above**) British infantrymen descending the ramps of a Landing Craft Infantry (LCI) transport at Reggio di Calabria on 3 September 1943, the start of Operation Baytown. During this amphibious operation, two divisions of the British Eighth Army's XIII Corps, the 1st Canadian and British 5th, crossed the Strait of Messina to capture Reggio di Calabria and advance up the toe of Italy. In addition to the two divisions, XIII Corps had attached to it an armoured unit and the 231st Independent (Malta) Infantry Brigade as well as some British and Royal Marine Commando units. (NARA)

(**Opposite, below**) Specialised landing craft, DUKWs, crossing the Strait of Messina with Canadian infantry, for landing at Reggio di Calabria on 3 September 1943. The American DUKW was derived from the GMC 6 × 6 truck, had a boat-shaped hull for buoyancy, and were both sturdy and reliable to transport troops, supplies and light weaponry from offshore to inland positions. Loading for Operation Baytown began on 31 August 1943 in Messina. (NARA)

(**Opposite, above**) Troops of the British 5th Division landing at Marina di Gallico in Calabria. DUKWs are being unloaded in the background. The infantryman in the centre is shouldering a Projector, Infantry Anti-Tank (PIAT) launcher, which had received its combat debut on Sicily. (*NARA*)

(**Opposite, below**) At Reggio di Calabria, on 3 September 1943, 1st Canadian Division infantrymen off-loading supplies from myriad types of landing craft including DUKWs, Landing Craft Mechanised (LCM) and Landing Craft Infantry (LCI). The Royal Air Force bombing sorties, Messina-based Royal Artillery and the Royal Navy's battleships *Nelson*, *Rodney*, *Warspite* and *Valiant* 16-inch gunfire prompted Montgomery's Chief of Staff, General Freddie de Guingand, to quip that the firepower support for Operation Baytown was like taking 'a sledgehammer to crack a nut'. (*NARA*)

(**Above**) Within the town of Reggio di Calabria, which fell uncontested to XIII Corps, three British servicemen are watching Italian troops, with their suitcases and gear neatly packed, march past after the unconditional surrender of 8 September 1943. Prior to the capitulation, Italian resistance was light and sometimes Italian soldiers even assisted with the off-loading of supplies. (*NARA*)

Infantrymen from the 1st Canadian Division passing through barbed wire as they march in single-file with full kit. These elements of the Eighth Army landed 200 miles to the south of the planned Fifth Army assault at Salerno, Operation Avalanche, on 9 September 1943. Amid those 200 miles were narrow, winding Calabrian roads as well as rugged areas of terrain to traverse, often with limited motor transport,. demolished roads and bridges, as well as booby traps and landmines left behind by the retreating LXXVI Panzer Corps. (NARA)

(**Opposite, above**) On 4 September 1943, British wounded from Calabria are being off-loaded from a Royal Navy lighter by Royal Army Medical Corps (RAMC) personnel at Messina. Despite an absence of enemy opposition, some British XIII Corps casualties were incurred from landmines and booby traps sown by the retreating German LXXVI Panzer Corps. (NARA)

(**Opposite, below**) Canadian troops queued up for canteen-filling from a water fountain in their northward Calabrian trek. The two divisions of British XIII Corps advanced from the beaches to their objective Catanzaro, 80 miles to the north, with the British 5th Division on the northern coast of the Italian toe and the Canadians on the southern side. The intense sun, heat and dust all added to the discomfort of the advancing Allied infantry, even though they were acclimated from the Sicilian Campaign. (NARA)

(**Opposite, above**) A column of British XIII Corps DUKWs, laden with supplies, moving northwards from Reggio di Calabria. In addition to the arduous trek, British quartermasters had initially allocated only enough supplies to reach Catanzaro, 80 miles inland. Despite the rough roads, enemy demolitions and mines, the Eighth Army with its tanks, guns, and trucks, averaged over 15 miles per day. (*NARA*)

(**Opposite, below**) British troops of the 5th Division's 17th Infantry Brigade marching along with an armoured column of M4 medium tanks and Universal carriers as they prepare to enter Nicastro, west of Tiriolo, near the Tyrrhenian coast of southern Italy. Prior to that march, from 3–8 September, units of the Royal Marine Commandos (No. 40), the 1st Special Raiding Squadron and elements of the British 13th and 15th Brigades of 5th Division made some offensive landings to get behind the retreating Germans on the Italian toe northern coastal locales at Bagnara, Gioia Tauro and San Venere. Elements of the 231st Independent (Malta) Brigade came to the aid of the Royal Marine Commandos that had landed at San Venere (near Pizzo) on 9 September and incurred over 200 casualties in combat with the retreating Germans of LXXVI Panzer Corps. (*NARA*)

(**Above**) Operation Slapstick commenced on 9 September 1943, with the amphibious assault by the British 1st Airborne Division (*above*) on the Italian naval base, which lies in the north-eastern end of the Gulf of Taranto. This was the same day as Operation Avalanche's launch in the Gulf of Salerno. This was an audacious strike for the 3,600 paratroopers, as they were entirely unsupported in enemy territory. Much of the Italian fleet had previously withdrawn or surrendered to the Allies the previous day. Although there was no direct enemy opposition, a troop-carrying vessel, HMS *Abdiel*, struck a mine and quickly sank with over 160 deaths including 120 paratroopers. (*Author's Collection*)

(**Above**) Royal Air Force service troops inspecting abandoned bombs and railcars in Taranto. Once ashore, the paratroopers of the 1st Airborne moved to the east and seized the airfield at Grottaglie. Then, separate units moved out to the north towards Bari and south-east to Brindisi, both on the Adriatic coast. (*NARA*)

(**Opposite, above**) A Landing Ship Tank (LST) with its bow ramps open at the Salerno shoreline on 9 September 1943. British 46th Division Universal carriers of the 6th Lincolnshire Regiment are moving over the rocky sand of Uncle Red Beach after disembarking from the ship's hull. This beach comprised the left flank of McCreery's X Corps' two infantry divisions, the 46th and 56th. German resistance consisted of the 16th Panzer Division at both the British beaches north of the Sele River and the American beaches south of the waterway. The Sele River was no more than a large stream. However, tanks and vehicles would not be able to cross it without bridging equipment. (*NARA*)

(**Opposite, below**) On 9 September 1943, a British truck is exiting from the hull of a Landing Ship Tank (LST), which had set up a protective smokescreen against enemy aircraft. The truck is moving over some burlap to give it added traction in the softer sand. From north to south, the British X Corps landing beaches were named Uncle Red, Uncle Green, Sugar Amber and Sugar Green for the 46th Division, as well as Roger Amber and Roger Green for the 56th Division. At the two Uncle beaches, the Nazis held two strongpoints, one called Lilienthal, was situated at the coast town of Magazzeno, while the other, Moltke, was located at the mouth of the Picentino River, which entered the Gulf of Salerno about a mile north of first position. The Royal Navy bombarded the previously built Italian fortifications at Lilienthal with rockets fired from converted Landing Craft Tank (LCT) vessels as well as naval gunfire, while British infantry outflanked the German 16th Panzer Division's defenders in the pillboxes and bunkers. It took approximately three-and-a-half hours after the 46th Division's 0330hrs assault to drive the Nazis inland. Later, McCreery set up X Corps headquarters near Magazzeno. (*NARA*)

(**Above**) American infantrymen of the 143rd regimental combat team (RCT) of the 36th Division coming ashore from their Landing Craft Personnel (LCP) in hip-deep water. This RCT was kept aboard ship as part of a floating reserve, along with the two RCTs of the US 45th Infantry Division, due to a lack of landing craft, during the early hours of Operation Avalanche's D-Day on the US VI Corps landing beaches Red, Green, Yellow, and Blue, and may explain the relative calm with which these troops are shown wading ashore. At these designated beach locales, the 141st and 142nd RCTs of the US 36th Infantry Division met with tenacious resistance by elements of the German 16th Panzer Division, which was the only enemy formation at the landing sites on D-Day. The American landing beaches stretched for 2 miles centred on the Hellenic ruins at Paestum. (*USAMHI*)

(**Opposite, above**) American infantrymen of the 143rd regimental combat team (RCT) of the 36th Division taking cover in s sand dunes at Red Beach as they await orders to move inland. Two battalions from each of the 141st and 142nd RCTs made the initial assaults at 0330hrs without any preliminary naval bombardment, since US VI Corps commanding general Dawley believed that stealth and rapid movement would overcome any resistance. However, heavy German gunfire from elements of the 16th Panzer Division pinned down both inexperienced RCTs of the Texas National Guard. Then German Panzers appeared just to the south of Paestum, approximately ninety minutes after the landings and actually reached the water's edge at the 141st RCT's Yellow and Blue beaches. It was to take almost an additional thirty minutes and the landing of the reserve battalions of both assaulting 36th Division RCTs to begin salvaging the shallow beachhead and compel the Nazi tanks to withdraw with timely use of recently dis-embarked self-propelled artillery and anti-aircraft (AA) guns. The 142nd RCT at Red and Green beaches contested Nazi machine-gun and sniper fire from Paestum's Greek ruins. Three hours after the initial assault waves landed, the 143rd RCT, which was held in reserve, landed to bolster the 142nd RCT at Paestum. (*USAMHI*)

(**Opposite, below**) British X Corps forces are shown consolidating one of their landing beaches north of the Sele River and to the town of Salerno's south during the afternoon of D-Day. A Landing Ship Tank (LST), with its bow ramps open, is seen at the shoreline (*left*), while a DUKW (*centre*) had some of its supplies unloaded for the British-crewed 40mm Bofors anti-aircraft (AA) gun emplacement (*right foreground*). Although the initial combat at the 46th Division's Uncle landing beaches had been fierce, the 56th Division's assault fared better. Infantry brigades from the 56th Division were able to advance across the Salerno Plain situated between the Tusciano and Asa rivers, in order to move north-east towards Battipaglia's railway facilities. As noon approached, other infantry brigades of the 56th Division reached the southern border of the Montecorvino airfield between the two rivers, which was an important British D-Day target. (*NARA*)

(**Opposite, above**) By the afternoon of D-Day, American M4 medium tanks, M10 tank destroyers, trucks and reinforcements continued to arrive despite the presence of German snipers and machine-gunfire. Although the beachhead was now secured after the Panzer threat hours before, Nazi artillery maintained steady bombardment of American positions all day. Elements of the German 16th Panzer Division had merely withdrawn in order to regroup for subsequent counter-attacks. (*NARA*)

(**Opposite, below**) A trio of US Rangers with their M1 Garand and Browning Automatic Rifles climbing over a small hill near the Chiunzi Pass on D-Day. The 4th Ranger battalions landed at 0320hrs on the Amalfi Coast at Maiori, a small fishing harbour. The 1st and 3rd Ranger battalions then came ashore with Colonel William O. Darby. The rangers quickly moved 6 miles inland to their objective, the Chiunzi Pass, by early morning, in addition to linking up with the Commandos of Brigadier Laycock's 2nd Special Service Brigade that had landed at Vietri, a few miles to the east. Holding the Chiunzi Pass was vital since the enemy moving along Highway 18 across the Sorrento Peninsula would have to traverse it to get to the beachhead and coastal roads to the town of Salerno. (*NARA*)

(**Above**) An American 75mm Howitzer firing a round in support of Darby's Rangers, who were struggling to hold the Chiunzi Pass from Nazi counter-attacks by the Hermann Göring Division. Since D-Day, the rangers had controlled the critical Chiunzi Pass and the Nocera defile, enabling them to directly observe Highway 18, which was the main supply route for the Germans to the northern part of the Salerno battlefield. There, the 83rd Chemical Battalion positioned 4.2-inch mortars to bombard the Nazi supply route. In addition to the 75mm Howitzer shown above, Darby had emplaced two naval forward observer parties. The Royal Navy's detachment directed HMS *Howe*, among other Allied ships, to also bombard the Nazis. The battle near the Chiunzi Pass raged for days, with elements of the ranger battalions moving inland well to the north of Amalfi to occupy heights above German positions at Gragnano and Castellamare to direct artillery fire on them. (*NARA*)

British troops of the 138th Infantry Brigade of the 46th Division disembarking unopposed into the town of Salerno during the morning hours on 10 September 1943, after it took several hours to clear German snipers and artillery snipers from this locale. By late morning, elements of the 46th Division's Reconnaissance Regiment established contact with Brigadier Laycock's 2nd Special Service Brigade that had landed at Vietri at 0330hrs the day before. (AWM)

German prisoners from the Hermann Göring Division are being marched to the rear through Vietri by a British Commando several days after Operation Avalanche commenced. Both British Army and Royal Marine Commandos from the 2nd Special Service Brigade landed at Vietri, a small fishing port located to the west of the town of Salerno on D-Day. The Germans were garbed in paratrooper knee-length smocks typical for this *Luftwaffe* formation. The Commandos secured Vietri on D-Day after some firefights with a German garrison, supported by a coastal battery, in the small port. Laycock's Commandos formed a vital defensive line on 13 September to defend against the long-awaited counter-attack by the Hermann Göring Division against the fishing village. Over 100 Commandos were lost in this action. (*Author's Collection*)

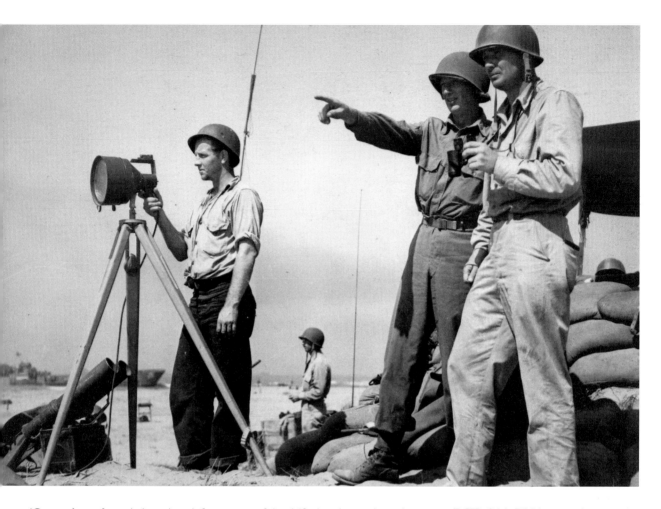

(**Opposite, above**) American infantrymen of the 143rd regimental combat team (RCT), 36th Division are shown entering Paestum on 9 September 1943. The four American beaches, which ran for 2 miles, was centred on this town, with the ruins just to the north. After the strong initial resistance mounted by the German 16th Panzer Division was overcome on D-Day, elements of this RCT were sent forward into the town, which would become the site of General Clark's Fifth Army headquarters. (*NARA*)

(**Opposite, below**) American infantrymen from the US 36th Division are shown rushing ashore from their assault craft on D-Day. This was probably a reinforcing wave as evidenced by the presence of matting material on the sand to facilitate the egress of vehicles off of the landing craft. (*NARA*)

(**Above**) A US Army captain is shown pointing offshore with a US Navy lieutenant holding binoculars in front of a sandbag-walled beachmaster's tent on one of the 36th Division's assigned beaches. A US Navy seaman on the far left signals messages to transports offshore to direct reinforcing supplies and reinforcements. German artillery, snipers, machine-gunfire, and aerial attack were all employed against the landing beaches making this position a precarious one throughout Operation Avalanche. (*NARA*)

(**Opposite, above**) A BeachMaster at the far right is shown directing supply and reinforcement unloading at one of the 36th Division's beaches near Paestum on D-Day, as the 143rd regimental combat team (RCT) arrived to bolster its division's other RCTs that had been reeling from an assault by the German 16th Panzer Division. In the background are DUKWs, with 105mm Howitzer pieces, self-propelled artillery. These weapons, along with infantry support weapons, enabled the beleaguered 141st RCTs to combat the tanks of the 16th Panzer Division during the morning hours of D-Day. (*USAMHI*)

(**Opposite, below**) A disabled German Mk IV Panzer is sitting idle within the Salerno, beached, as a testimony to the failed tank assault launched by the German 16th Panzer Division from the Albanella Station against the 36th Division's 141st and 142nd regimental combat teams (RCTs) on D-Day. Other American military vehicles, such as a DUKW and two C-47 transport planes, are shown within the beachhead suggesting that this photograph was taken at a later stage during the Salerno invasion. (*NARA*)

(**Above**) Royal Navy warships and transports are seen offshore from the British X Corps beaches as an explosion erupts in the left background, probably from a *Luftwaffe* bombing or Nazi-guided aerial bomb. The British 46th and 56th divisions assaulted under the cover of a naval bombardment of the beaches with rocket barrages and targets inland with the heavy guns of the Royal Navy's battleships *Warspite* and *Valiant* among, other combat vessels. (*USAMHI*)

(**Above**) A pair of American soldiers scanning the sky from their DUKW-mounted .50-inch calibre anti-aircraft (AA) machine-gun, as German aerial assaults were a ubiquitous danger. Larger Landing Ship Tank (LST) and smaller Landing Craft Infantry (LCI) transports are shown at the shoreline (*background*) and provided enticing targets to Nazi aircraft. During the initial three days of Operation Avalanche, *Luftflotte* 2 launched more than 450 sorties by fighters and fighter-bombers, and almost 100 heavy bombers, against the invasion fleet. (*NARA*)

(**Opposite, above**) Tracer bullets from Allied warships offshore illuminated the night-time sky during a Nazi aerial attack. XIV Panzer Corps commander Balck wanted the *Luftwaffe* to concentrate on the warships rather than against the Allied ground forces, as the Allied battle fleet was wreaking havoc on the German counter-attacks with accurate naval gunfire. (*NARA*)

(**Opposite, below**) American troops are shown examining the wreck of a Nazi fighter, with its distinctively painted propeller, on the beach at Paestum. German pilots sunk four transports, one heavy cruiser and seven landing craft as well as making more than eighty other hits on Allied shipping. Success was also observed with the new Nazi radio-controlled glider bombs that were carried by Dornier and Heinkel bombers before release onto their targets. On 11 September 1943, damage was incurred by USS *Philadelphia*, and USS *Savannah* was put out of action by these new types of German ordnance. With these losses, additional Royal Navy cruisers were dispatched from Malta to the Gulf of Salerno for fire-support missions. (*NARA*)

(**Opposite, above**) A downed American Spitfire Mk IX fighter of the US 307th Fighter Squadron is shown disabled along the shoreline near a Landing Ship Tank (LST) offloading its vehicles via a pontoon to reinforce the beachhead later on 9 September 1943. This fighter squadron covered the Allied armada and landing beaches for Operation Avalanche. On 23 September, the US 307th Fighter Squadron moved to Montecorvino Airfield after its capture. On 13 October, the squadron moved to an all-weather airfield at Pomigliano, 9 miles to the north-east of Naples, as the mud and craters at Montecorvino precluded safe landing and take-offs. (*NARA*)

(**Above**) American troops aboard Landing Ship Tank (LST) transport vessels watching where *Luftwaffe* bombs are falling during the Nazi aerial assault on the Salerno beachhead. Ships of all types were targeted in the Gulf of Salerno by the German pilots and pilotless guided aerial bombs. US Navy shipping losses were numerous and diverse. The Royal Navy lost five LCTs and the hospital ship *Newfoundland*, despite the insignia of the Red Cross being prominently displayed. (*NARA*)

(**Opposite, below**) The American cruiser USS *Savannah* is seen after the ship was struck by a Nazi radio-controlled guided bomb. Although the Germans had this weapon ready for use for the Sicily invasion, Hitler deferred its surprise use until the Italian mainland was assaulted. These pilotless bombs were fitted with wings and assisted by rockets. Radio control or a homing device directed them. The bombs, less than 20in in diameter and weighing over 600lb, were capable of piercing a warship's armour plating and possessed a delayed fuse. (*USAMHI*)

(**Above**) A wounded American infantryman is being evacuated by US Navy corpsmen onto a Landing Craft Vehicle, Personnel (LCVP) after being injured on the beachhead at Salerno. *(USAMHI)*

(**Opposite**) A German Stug III Ausf G assault gun with a 75mm Stu K 40 anti-tank (AT) gun is shown. This self-propelled gun (SPG) was based on the chassis of the Panzer Mk III. On the Allied left flank in the British X Corps sector, a XIV Panzer Corps *kampfgruppe* with a company of these SPGs and a reconnaissance battalion of the 16th Panzer Division was launched during the night of 10–11 September 1943. They were met by elements of the British 46th Division's 139th Brigade. A paucity of good roads hampered the Nazi armoured thrust. However, the British were forced to retreat. Disaster was averted when the entire complement of the 46th Division's artillery fired on the enemy with the added support of Royal Navy gunfire. *(USAMHI)*

(**Opposite, above**) A British 7th Armoured Division M4 medium tank is disabled by a German anti-tank (AT) gun. This armoured formation was one of the main Allied reinforcements to help secure the Salerno beachhead. This British armoured division had seen almost three years of combat in North Africa and was highly experienced. By 14 September 1943, the transports carrying this formation had arrived offshore to reinforce the two British X Corps divisions, both of which had been under fierce Nazi counter-attack. The deployment of the 7th Armoured Division on 15 September aided the British 56th Division's exposed right flank in the vicinity of the Fosso Bridge along the Tusciano River. (*USAMHI*)

(**Opposite, below**) An Allied M4 medium tank is seen passing a disabled German Mk IV Panzer with additional side armour lost during the repeated counter-attacks against the US VI Corps beachhead. The main threat to the 36th Division's initial two regimental combat teams (RCTs) on 9 September 1943 were the Mk IV Panzers of the 16th Panzer Division that had extended to near the shoreline before American tanks could land. The most severe threat occurred at 1000hrs on D-Day, when thirteen Panzers were observed approaching Paestum. Naval gunfire, aerial fighter-bomber attack, a few American self-propelled artillery pieces and infantry support weapons managed to drive the Nazis off with five enemy Panzers lost before their retreat. The tenacious defence mounted by the German Tenth Army at Salerno, especially by its 16th Panzer Division early on, was coupled with armoured counter-offensives by both the remaining two Nazi XIV Panzer Corps divisions as well as northwardly retiring LXXIV Panzer Corps formations to the west and south of the town of Salerno, respectively. (*NARA*)

(**Above**) A Panzer VI Tiger disabled by an American infantry anti-tank gun. The Panzer VI entered service in August 1942 and, although it was an excellent combat armoured vehicle, it was difficult to produce in large numbers and hard to maintain in the field. An overlapping wheel suspension was prone to malfunction from caked mud, which was common during the Italian Campaign. The Panzer VI first saw action against the British in Tunisia in late 1942. (*USAMHI*)

(**Above**) Dead German soldiers lying along the roadside near Altavilla near Hill 424 to the south-east of Persano and the heavily contested Tobacco Factory in the US VI sector after the Nazi counter-attacks. The Allied planners, in establishing the initial objectives for Operation Avalanche, had included the high ground near Altavilla, specifically Hill 424. If the British X Corps were to seize the heights at Battipaglia and Eboli, the British and American rendezvous at Ponte Sele was to effectively seal off the Sele-Calore Plain. However, the German counter-attacks against the separated British X and US VI Corps sectors nullified this invasion plan. On 12 September, the 15th Panzergrenadier Regiment of the 29th Panzer Grenadier Division struck across Hill 424, which caused elements of the US 36th Division's 142nd Infantry Regiment to withdraw towards Altavilla. General Walker, commanding general of the 36th Division, had to commit four of his seven available infantry battalions as the conflict for Altavilla intensified. However, Nazi control of Hill 424 above the town prevented the American capture of this locale. (*NARA*)

(**Opposite**) An American infantryman examining a captured German infantry dugout near a wrecked Flak 88 anti-aircraft (AA) anti-tank (AT) gun of the Nazi 16th Panzer Division, which resisted the invasion across the broad frontage of beaches in both the US VI and British X Corps sectors. In one such action, Sergeant Manuel Gonzales, of Company F of the US 36th Division's 142nd regimental combat team (RCT), spotted a German 88 firing from the dunes towards the landing craft of a subsequent assault wave. After he killed the German gun-crew with hand-grenades, he blew up the remaining enemy ammunition for the weapon. Meeting the Allied assault troops on D-Day, the German 16th Panzer Division contained more than 100 tanks, 17,000 men and thirty-six assault guns. On 9 September 1943, the tanks from the 16th Panzer Division swung into action just after daylight. (*NARA*)

General Mark Clark, the Fifth Army commander, talking to American VI Corps soldiers. He congratulated them for their contribution at stiffening up the US VI Corps sector during the crisis of Black Monday, 13 September 1943, after their late evening paratroop drop. (NARA)

A British M4 medium tank from the Royal Scots Greys attached to the 56th Division of X Corps during the fighting along the Tusciano River. The tank, with some attached infantry, was moving across some railway tracks towards the Fosso Bridge. The camouflage scheme utilised by the tank was one that had been employed by the regiment during its combat in Tunisia earlier in 1943. Smoke from an Allied wreckage at the beachhead is seen in the background. On 11 September 1943, a Nazi armoured thrust directly along the railway line south of Battipaglia broke the 8th Battalion Royal Fusiliers' defence and, as this formation retreated towards the Fosse Bridge, many of the fleeing 56th Division infantrymen were killed or captured by the Germans. Timely use of divisional artillery targeted the southern approaches of the Fosse Bridge and prevented its capture by the enemy. (NARA)

An American Jeep convoy with infantry of the US 3rd Division moves off the beaches after landing at Paestum on 18 September 1943, five days after the Nazi counter-attacks by LXXVI Panzer Corps on Black Monday. On that critical day, General Mark Clark had even contemplated evacuating the US VI Corps beachhead and moving Dawley's American troops into the British X Corps sector. After the Germans over-ran an American infantry battalion at the Tobacco Factory near Persano, only a thin line of General Dawley's VI Corps artillery and anti-tank (AT) guns was situated on the far bank of the Calore River as it converged with the Sele River. In addition to the AT fire, American engineers destroyed bridges over the Calore River to prevent the Germans from seizing them for the Panzers to cross the waterway. A few days later, during the evening of 18 September, elements of the US 45th Infantry Division re-occupied the Tobacco Factory. By 19 September, Persano was recaptured by US 36th Division infantry. Also, on that day, the US VI Corps commander, Major-General Dawley, was relieved of his command by Clark. (*NARA*)

A Universal carrier of the British 56th Division entering the ruins of Battipaglia on 18 September 1943. By dawn of D-Day +1, British 56th Division's 9th Battalion Royal Fusiliers had entered Battipaglia. Strong elements of the German 16th Panzer Division counter-attacked, which caused some of the British infantry battalion to retreat from this railway town, while others were forced to surrender. For just over a week, heavy fighting raged along the banks of the Tusciano River before the British were able to re-enter Battipaglia. (NARA)

Chapter Five

Allied Advances to the Gustav Line and Stalemate

As the battles along the Gulf of Salerno were drawing to a close, along Italy's Adriatic coast, units of the British Eighth Army continued to move north. On 18 September, British V Corps headquarters, under Lieutenant-General Charles W. Allfrey, arrived at Taranto and received the British 78th Division at Bari. On 20 September, Canadian contingents of the Eighth Army occupied Potenza, 50 miles to the east of Salerno, and linked up with the British 1st Airborne Division, the latter having already taken Taranto and Brindisi during Operation Slapstick. Montgomery's next objective was to be the airdrome complex at Foggia, which was taken by converging British and Canadian forces on 1 October. This complex of airfields was to become the base from which Allied bombers assaulted targets in Austria, southern Germany and other sites in the Balkans.

McCreery's X Corps was to move up Italy's Tyrrhenian coast around Monte Vesuvius to arrive onto the Naples plain. Coincident with this movement, Lucas's VI Corps was to advance north-westward through the mountains to protect the British right flank. By 30 September, X Corps forces reached the outskirts of Naples and continued northwards. The following day, 1 October, Naples was liberated by elements of the US 82nd Airborne Division and Darby's Rangers, both units acting under McCreery's leadership. However, the capture of Naples was initially disappointing as both the city and port had been thoroughly destroyed by Allied bombardment, German demolition and the intentional sinking of ships in the harbour. Nonetheless, the port was re-opened for shipping traffic within a week of its capture, despite persistent German air-raids.

By 7 October, X Corps reached the Volturno River, to the south of Capua, in force with the Germans on the northern bank behind the natural terrain barrier. The VI Corps northern advance had been hampered by thorough Nazi demolition of bridges and steep mountain ranges, and waterways with rapid currents. The rugged nature of the terrain necessitated the use of mules for transport as well as the spanning of rivers with Bailey bridges. By 7 October, after advancing over 60 miles through this inland region, VI Corps, comprising the US 45th and newly arrived 3rd and

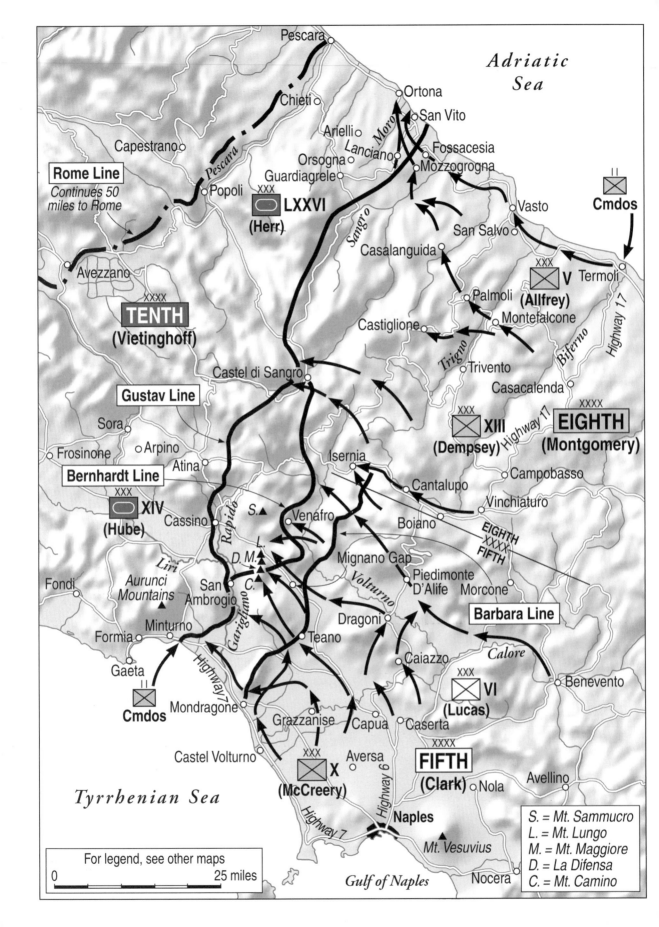

Pescara

*Adriatic
Sea*

Ortona
San Vito
Arielli
Lanciano
Fossacesia
Mozzogrogna
Orsogna
Guardiagrele
Vasto
Chieti
San Salvo

Rome Line
*Continues 50
miles to Rome*

Capestrano

Popoli

XXX
LXXVI
(Herr)

Casalanguida

Casalenda

Cmdos

V
(Allfrey) Termoli

Avezzano

Palmoli
Montefalcone

TENTH
(Vietinghoff)

Castiglione
Trivento

Trigno

Casacalenda

Biferno

Highway 17

Castel di Sangro

Gustav Line

Sora

Isernia

XIII
(Dempsey)

EIGHTH
(Montgomery)

Campobasso

Cantalupo

Vinchiaturo

Arpino

Bernhardt Line

Frosinone

Atina

XXX
XIV
(Hube) Cassino

S.▲

Venafro

Boiano

EIGHTH
XXXX
FIFTH

Fondi

Liri

Rapido

L.▲
D. M.▲
▲
C.

Mignano Gap

Piedimonte
D'Alife

Morcone

*Aurunci
Mountains*
▲

San
Ambrogio

Volturno

Barbara Line

Minturno

Formia

Dragoni

Gaeta

Garigliano

Teano

Caiazzo

Calore

Benevento

Cmdos Mondragone

Grazzanise

Capua

Caserta

XXX
VI
(Lucas)

Castel Volturno

XXX
X
(McCreery)

Aversa

FIFTH
(Clark) Nola

Avellino

Tyrrhenian Sea

Highway 7

Highway 6

Naples

▲
Mt. Vesuvius

Nocera

For legend, see other maps

0   25 miles

Gulf of Naples

S. = Mt. Sammucro
L. = Mt. Lungo
M. = Mt. Maggiore
D. = La Difensa
C. = Mt. Camino

34th divisions, reached the southern bank of the Volturno River. Both the X and VI Corps attacked across the Volturno River on 13–14 October, as Allied artillery opened fire along the front mixing smoke shells and high explosives to screen the crossing sites. A few minutes before the artillery was scheduled to lift, infantrymen slogged through muddy fields to reach the river after carrying assault boats and ferry sections for the crossing.

General von Vietinghoff placed the 35,000 men of the XIV Panzer Corps along the north bank of the Volturno River. Stretching from the Tyrrhenian coast at Castel Volturno and extending inland were the 15th Panzer Grenadier, the remaining battalions of the Hermann Göring, the 3rd Panzer Grenadier, and a reconnaissance battalion from the 26th Panzer divisions. These veteran Nazi formations were situated directly in front of the two Fifth Army corps, the latter attacking abreast, each comprising three divisions. To the west of the Volturno, as the river made its northward bend and extending to the Adriatic coast, was the German LXXVI Panzer Corps, comprising the major portion of the 26th Panzer, the 29th Panzer Grenadier, the 1st Parachute and 16th Panzer divisions.

Five battalions of General Truscott's US 3rd Division crossed the Volturno River and secured their objectives by the afternoon of 13 October with an improvised ferry service. By the morning of 14 October, the US 3rd Division crushed the left flank of the Hermann Göring Division and created a bridgehead 4 miles deep. Combat engineers, under fire, erected light pontoon bridges for infantry and a heavier 8-ton bridge for vehicles, all needing maintenance and near constant re-fitting due to enemy artillery fire. A 30-ton bridge for armour was also constructed on 14 October. The 3rd Division's *coup de main* crossing of the Volturno River resulted in only approximately 400 total casualties. The US 34th and 45th divisions also crossed the Volturno, despite opposition from the German 3rd Panzer Grenadier Division, which Vietinghoff did not hold in high esteem.

Allied Fifth (under Clark) and Eighth (under Montgomery) armies' advances and German defences, mid-October 1943 through to January 1944. Natural terrain features, such as the numerous Italian rivers, the Volturno, Garigliano and Rapido, in the Fifth Army (British X and US VI corps) zone and the Biferno, Trigno, and Sangro along the Eighth Army (British XIII and V corps) Front, as well as mountain complexes, such as those along the Montes Camino–la Difensa–Maggiore–Lungo–Sammucro chain and the Apennines, were now to be force multipliers for General Vietinghoff's German Tenth Army's XIV (under Hube) and LXXVI (under Herr) Panzer corps to contest Allied movements across the waist of the Italian Peninsula. Despite successful Allied crossings of many of these terrain barriers, the Allied 15th Army Group (under Alexander) advances towards Cassino and into the Liri Valley as well as beyond the Rome Line were thwarted by tenacious German formations manning the constructed defences of Kesselring's Winter Line, comprising the Barbara, Bernhardt and Gustav lines. To sustain both the Allied Fifth and Eighth armies' advances, numerous reinforcing divisions from many countries were to be dispatched to both army sectors (see text for details) on either side of the Apennines. (*Philip Schwartzberg, Meridian Mapping, Minneapolis, MN*)

Following up on the success of the US 3rd Division attack, the British 56th Division had only one road in its immediate sector, which crossed the Volturno River at Capua. The British 7th Armoured Division was to also cross via a single country road at Grazzanise. The British 46th Division was to make its river assault near Castel Volturno, but since the Germans had destroyed the bridges over the river, this formation had to traverse the waterway utilising several Landing Craft Tanks to ferry a tank company around the mouth of the river under Allied naval gunfire cover on 13 October. Infantry battalions of the 46th Division then paddled across the river and resisted Nazi counter-attacks on their bridgehead. By the evening of 15 October, the forward companies of this division were 4 miles inland beyond the Volturno. The crossing of the Volturno by the British 56th Division near Capua came under strong enemy artillery fire and was deemed not feasible. It had to be relocated to an area spanned by a bridge across the waterway that had been constructed by the US 3rd Division. By the afternoon of 14 October, the troops and vehicles of the British 56th Division crossed the bridge above Triflisco. McCreery's X Corps had incurred over 600 casualties in the river's crossing by his three divisions.

General von Vietinghoff had abided by Kesselring's timetable and held the Volturno River fortifications with Hube's XIV Panzer Corps until 15 October, when he ordered a fighting withdrawal northward, which was to limit the Fifth Army's advance to 15–20 miles north of the river over the next several days during this month. Then, XIV Panzer Corps was to continue its orderly retreat into the mountainous terrain that contained the Barbara and Bernhardt lines.

On the Adriatic coast of Italy, Montgomery next turned towards a new terrain goal, the Biferno River and sent XIII Corps troops along the coastal road to the port and town of Termoli. This port was reached with an amphibious operation that utilised British Commandos initially, which were subsequently reinforced by elements of the British 78th Division on 3 October. Then, three days of intense infantry and tank fighting ensued with the counter-attacking German 16th Panzer Division, during which several Mk IV Panzers were destroyed by Canadian tankers of the Three Rivers Regiment.

After his successes at Foggia and Termoli, Montgomery reorganised his front on 9 October, assigning the Adriatic coastal area to Alfrey's V Corps, comprising the British 78th and Indian 8th divisions. The New Zealand 2nd Division, under Freyberg, was due to arrive soon in Taranto and join V Corps. In addition, the Eighth Army on its coastal drive had the British 4th Armoured and 2nd Special Service Brigades. The XIII Corps was responsible for an interior zone with the Canadian 1st and British 5th divisions. The Eighth Army paused on 9 October along a line stretching from Termoli to Campobasso, for re-supply and reinforcements. The Canadians occupied Campobasso, well to the west of the Adriatic coast, on 14 October after the Germans had withdrawn after heavy fighting with much destruction of the city.

The formidable LXXVI Panzer Corps opposed the Eighth Army along the Trigno River by the end of October. The German 16th Panzer and 29th Panzer Grenadier divisions guarded the coastal sector, with the German 1st Parachute Division immediately to its south. Montgomery's initial successes at Foggia and Termoli made it necessary to move the German 26th Panzer Division into the Adriatic sector to bolster the Nazi divisions already there.

The 78th Division started the attack on the coast on 27 October 1943 but was repulsed by resistance from the 16th Panzer Division. The XIII Corps offensive was postponed by bad weather, and it was not until the night of 29–30 October that the Canadians struck at the 26th Panzer Division's positions and took Cantalupo on 1 November. Although the 8th Indian Division received a sharp repulse at Tuffilo on 2 November, a battalion of the British 78th Division crossed the Trigno River on 4 November and captured the village of San Salvo from the 16th Panzer Division, and the following day took Vasto. By 5 November, the Canadians had taken the important road junction at Isernia. The German LXXVI Panzer Corps was forced to retreat to the Sangro River, where the German 65th Infantry Division was constructing field fortifications. The terrain beyond the Trigno River had a few miles of flat farmland, which was suitable for tank movement. However, cold torrential rain turned this area into a muddy obstacle to penetrate. The delay inflicted on the Eighth Army's movements by weather and stout Nazi resistance along the Adriatic had enabled the completion of the Gustav Line fortifications as well as those on the Sangro River.

In order for the Eighth Army to reach the Rome Line, Montgomery had to advance as far as Pescara on the Adriatic coast north of both the Sangro River and Ortona. Italy's Adriatic winter was quite severe and movement on the eastern side of the snow-capped mountains treacherous. The weather and mud-induced delay gave Kesselring pause to move the German 26th Panzer and 29th Panzer Grenadier divisions back west across the peninsula to combat the Fifth Army on the Bernhardt Line. Thus, Montgomery had to face only the German 65th Infantry Division on the lower Sangro and the 1st Parachute Division in the middle and upper parts of the river. The British 78th Division had only arrived at the lower reaches of the Sangro River by 8 November and bad weather produced another pause in the fighting. Any thoughts of entering Rome by the end of the year seemed to rapidly dwindle as Montgomery, after the delay which enabled the Germans to further fortify their positions, had to first secure the high ridge and fortified villages of Mozzogrogna and Fossacesia that had overlooked the Sangro River and then take Ortona.

On 20 November 1943, Montgomery resumed his Eighth Army offensive and had the British 78th Division's 36th Brigade cross the lower Sangro River. More units continued to cross such that, by 22 November, five battalions of the 78th Division had established an enlarged bridgehead. British engineers made tracks out of the mud with bulldozers and erected Bailey bridges, such that by 27 November approximately a hundred tanks of the British 4th Armoured Brigade were across the Sangro River. On 28 November, Gurkhas of the 17th Indian Brigade captured Mozzogrogna. However, with the armour delayed by demolished bridges, the German 65th Infantry Division supported by *Nebelwerfers* and a Panzer detachment forced them to withdraw. Now with some good weather, Fossacesia was captured by British armour and infantry on 30 November. By the evening of 4 December, the British 78th Division's 36th Brigade had reached the Moro River, just south of Ortona and well to the north of the Sangro River. There, the advancing Eighth Army units clashed with elements of the German 90th Panzer Grenadier Division that Kesselring had dispatched from Sardinia to relieve the shattered German 65th Infantry Division and staunch Montgomery's Adriatic advance. In addition to the German 90th Panzer Grenadier and 1st Parachute divisions, Kesselring employed both the 15th Panzer Grenadier and 26th Panzer divisions as well as the 334th Infantry Division brought south from Genoa.

During the last week of November 1943, the Canadians were transferred to the V Corps on the Adriatic coast. Fanatical German paratrooper resistance with expert bridge and road demolition slowed the V Corps advance north of the Sangro River on the Adriatic coast. Elements of the German 90th Panzer Grenadier Division clashed with a brigade of the 1st Canadian Division on a ridge north of the Moro River and astride the Ortona–Orsogna road. The German paratroopers were positioned now between Berardi and the sea and the *panzergrenadiers* were spread out to the west for about 4,000 yards, thus forming a compact and continuous front against the Canadians, who took the crossroads west of Berardi on 20 December. The *panzergrenadiers* were forced back into the town of Ortona, where defences were being prepared for street-fighting. Montgomery hoped to utilise Ortona as a port. However, German demolitions and booby traps rather than Allied bombardment, produced numerous rock-strewn barricades to repel Canadian infantry and armour. The German 1st Parachute Division was moved into Ortona to take over for the badly mauled 90th Panzer Grenadier Division.

The stubborn defence by the German paratroopers produced a week of savage fighting for the Canadians for Ortona. Major-General Chris Vokes, in command of the Canadian 1st Division, had ordered a massive artillery bombardment of the Nazi positions on 24 December. However, it was not until three days later that a patrol of the Princess Patricia's Canadian Light Infantry managed to break into the devastated town. The surviving German paratroopers then withdrew a couple of miles to a prepared position in the rear.

Elsewhere on the Adriatic Front during December 1943, elements of the Indian 8th Division forced its way into Tollo, another coastal Italian town destroyed by bombardment. The 2nd New Zealand Division also had to contend with fanatical Nazi opposition at the villages of Orsogna and Guardiagrele, both of which had been converted into major strongpoints defended by elements of the German 26th Panzer Division. Despite a combination of XIII Corps artillery and V Corps infantry formations, German General von Lüttwitz's 26th Panzer Division still held Orsogna by 23 December, although Arielli to the north-east was captured by the 15th Brigade of the British 5th Division.

Eventually, Montgomery, who departed for England on 27 December, fell short of his objective. Although the Eighth Army had advanced beyond the Sangro and Moro rivers, Chieti and Pescara, the latter being the Adriatic coast anchor of the Rome Line north of Ortona, remained in German hands. The Eighth Army was forced to halt its offensive just north of the Orsogna–Ortona Line.

On 5 November 1943, X Corps turned towards Montes Camino, la Difensa, and Maggiore, stretching about 8 miles as a mountain chain. Two British 56th Division brigades were tasked with the scaling of the steep Monte Camino, 3,000 feet above the Garigliano Valley. The waiting 15th Panzer Grenadier Division had constructed fortifications of barbed wire, booby traps and weapon pits. Three Nazi counter-attacks on 8 November failed to hurl the British off the mountain from their shallow rocky positions halfway up the massif. However, bad weather, exhaustion, limited rations and ammunition, and mounting numbers of wounded compelled the British abandonment of Monte Camino by 14 November.

US VI Corps, with the 3rd, 34th and 45th divisions, along with the 504th PIR of the 82nd Airborne Division, also had a difficult time fighting in the mountains after crossing the Volturno River in an area stretching from the Mignano Gap in the west through Venafro and Isernia to the east. These operations began on 31 October when one of the 3rd Division's regiments was ordered to scale the almost perpendicular face of Monte la Difensa. However, after ten days of combat and harsh weather, they were unsuccessful. The VI Corps commander Lucas stated, 'Wars should be fought in better country than this.' The remaining regiments of the 3rd Division were more successful as they smashed through the Nazi fortifications comprising the Barbara Line, and took Monte Rotondo and part of Monte Lungo, both heights flanking Highway 6 north of Mignano. Kesselring feared that his forces, which had been fighting on the defensive and in retreat since North Africa, would falter in the face of the British 56th Division fighting at Monte Camino and the US 3rd Division taking territory near Mignano.

On 13 November, the Fifth Army's offensive came to a halt as Clark informed Alexander about the state of his attacking divisions. On 15 November, Alexander halted the attacks to allow the Fifth Army to rest for two weeks. With some units having left the MTO for England, principally the British 7th Armoured and the US 82nd Airborne divisions (less the 504th PIR), for training for the Normandy invasion and with additional reinforcements not yet having arrived, the fortnight's respite enabled Clark's two corps to regroup and refit in the face of bad weather and troop exhaustion.

Kesselring's formations did not crumble nor were any cut off from the orderly withdrawal. Allied planners focused on upcoming operations at the Garigliano and Rapido rivers to gain access into the Liri Valley as the pathway to Rome. Geopolitically, an Allied capture of the Eternal City would demonstrate to the Soviets that the Allied Italian Campaign constituted a Second Front in the West. There were also airfield complexes near Rome for continued Allied bombing of the Nazi heartland.

In mid-November 1943, Lieutenant-General Keyes' II Corps headquarters moved from Sicily into the line between the X and VI corps, with the US 3rd and 36th divisions as its nucleus. Also, as Italy had declared war on Germany as a cobelligerent, the small Italian First Motorised Group joined the Fifth Army. Other additional formations included: the US 1st Armoured Division; the regimental-sized elite mountain-trained troops of the Canadian-American 1st Special Service Force (SSF); and General Juin's French Expeditionary Corps (FEC), comprising the 2nd Moroccan and 3rd Algerian divisions. These new formations were to augment the number of Allied divisions campaigning in Italy to fourteen by the end of 1943 and beginning of January 1944.

Over on the Tyrrhenian coast, after a two-week hiatus, the X Corps offensive resumed on the night of 1 – 2 December, as the British 46th Division took Calabritto. The main attack commenced during the afternoon of 2 December, when over 900 British guns fired continuously on Monte Camino and adjacent hills against the 15th Panzer Grenadier Division. Over 200,000 shells were released in the largest concentration of firepower in the Italian Campaign. During the early hours of 3 December, Allied troops attacked Mount Camino with elements of the British 56th and 46th divisions approaching from the south, while II Corps, spearheaded by US Rangers, the 1st SSF, and a regiment from the US 36th Division, stormed the mountain from the eastern side. The battle raged for a few days and, by 6 December, the Allies finally controlled Monte Camino and the southern pillar of the Mignano Pass along that portion of the Bernhardt Line.

Frederick's Canadian–American 1st SSF was trained for harsh winter mountain combat after making their debut spearheading an American amphibious landing on Kiska in the Aleutian Islands. This elite unit made a night-time climbing assault on Monte la Difensa on 1 December and reached the summit by dawn. Horrific combat ensued on the mountaintop, with Nazi resistance ending on 8 December as the US 36th Division seized Monte Maggiore.

A corps force comprising the 142nd Infantry Regiment of the 36th Division and the First Italian Motorised Brigade, in its anti-Nazi combat debut, attacked Monte Lungo on 7 December, immediately to the north beyond the Montes Camino/la Difensa/

Maggiore massif. The Italians suffered grievously under withering German artillery fire by the 29th Panzer Grenadier Division. A separate attack on Monte Sammucro, the northern pillar of the Mignano Pass overlooking the village of San Pietro, was made on 8 December. Monte Sammucro and San Pietro were held by strong German elements of the XIV Panzer Corps' 15th Panzer Grenadier and 71st Infantry divisions. The ten-day tenacious Nazi defence at San Pietro, beginning on 8 December, embroiled the US 36th Division's 143rd Infantry Regiment, the US 3rd Ranger Battalion, the 504th PIR and a company of American M4 tanks and M10 tank destroyers from the 753rd Tank Battalion. After nearby Monte Lungo was taken by other II Corps units after a renewed attack on 15 December, San Pietro's Nazi defenders withdrew fearing severance of their line of retreat. US 36th Division troops entered a ruined San Pietro on 17 December.

The VI Corps, now comprising the 34th and 45th divisions, on the right of the Fifth Army attacked German XIV Panzer Corps troops as a supporting operation for the Eighth Army's efforts on the Sangro Front. These American divisions assaulted to the west of the Bernhardt Line's salient created by the mountainous pillars of the Mignano Gap. The formidable XIV Panzer Corps units and the mountainous terrain halted the Americans' effort to turn the German left flank north of Highway 6. However, the US 45th Division along with the 2nd Moroccan Infantry Division, the latter having taken over the US 34th Division's sector on 12 December, seized Monte Pantano from the German 305th Infantry Division after five days of combat. On 22 December, elements of the US 45th Division succeeded in taking the commanding height of Monte Cavallo. With the US 3rd Division, the 45th, was pulled out of the line for the Anzio operation.

With the advent of January 1944, it was II Corps' 34th and 36th divisions along with the FEC 2nd Moroccan and 3rd Algerian divisions that kept up pressure on the Germans north of Cassino and Highway 6. Slowly, the XIV Panzer Corps was forced back onto the Gustav Line and across the Rapido River.

Lieutenant-General Oliver Leese had taken over the command of the Eighth Army with Montgomery's departure. Eisenhower also left the MTO for England and Supreme Command for the Normandy operation. General Sir Henry Maitland Wilson, who had been campaigning in the Middle East, North Africa and Greece since 1940, became commander-in-chief Allied Forces Mediterranean with the American Lieutenant-General Jacob Devers his deputy.

On 16 January 1944, II Corps had secured Monte Trocchio, the last high ground before the Rapido River, to the south-west of Cassino. This vantage point gave the Allies a commanding view of the positions held by the German 44th Division. Clark decided to assault the Gustav Line to get into the Liri Valley from the south, which was barred by the fast-flowing waterway formed by the Rapido, Garigliano and Liri rivers. The II Corps crossing of the Rapido with the 36th Division was planned to enable the US 1st Armoured Division to break out beyond the far bank. Simultaneous with the American assault across the Rapido River, X Corps, now strengthened on 15 January with the British 5th Division moving west from the Adriatic Front, was scheduled to cross the Garigliano River near the coast to the south-west through the Aurunci Mountains towards the Liri Valley.

McCreery's X Corps had more than a month to rest its 56th and 46th divisions along with its armoured support and to reconnoiter the Garigliano crossings. On the evening of 17 January, X Corps artillery fired across the Garigliano River, while Allied ships in the Gulf of Gaeta pounded German positions to the rear of the river's northern bank. The Nazis did not recoil. The British 5th Division crossed the river across the narrow estuary in landing craft around the Garigliano's mouth and then moved on Minturno and Tufo at the entrance to the Ausente valley. The British 56th Division successfully crossed the river and attacked through the positions of the German 276th Grenadier Regiment towards Castelforte. The British 46th Division attempted the river crossing on either side of Sant' Ambrogio, just to the south of the confluence of the Rapido, Liri and Garigliano rivers, where it would serve as the left flank of the II Corps. The 46th Division's river assault fared poorly under enemy fire, was turned back at every point, and had to be postponed until the next day. By the morning of 18 January, all of the British 5th and 56th divisions' attacking formations were across the river and had established bridgeheads after compelling the German 94th Infantry Division in the foothills of the northern bank to retreat. The 46th Division was moved south of the abortive crossing of Sant' Ambrogio to join the British 5th and 56th divisions and be employed as X Corps would now defend against Nazi counter-attacks.

As the Garigliano River was being assaulted by the X Corps, II Corps engineers were clearing minefields on the approaches to the Rapido River north of the Liri River. Under the cover of darkness, the 36th Division was also bringing forward assault boats, bridging equipment, ammunition and smoke pots, the latter to help mask the upcoming river crossing from the overlooking German positions. However, by the night of 20 January, the American attempts to clear mines and mark paths to the river's edge were inadequate. The Rapido River assault, which began on the night of 20 January, ended in disaster for Walker's 36th Division. By the morning of 21 January, only a handful of platoons from the 143rd Infantry Regiment had managed to cross to the south of Sant'Angelo in Theodice and tenuously held a portion of the river's western bank. After a German counter-attack, the assaulting elements of the regiment's 1st Battalion had to retreat back across the river under enemy fire. To the north of Sant' Angelo in Theodice, two companies from the 141st Infantry Regiment of the 36th established a small bridgehead, but it too proved impossible to strongly reinforce as only a total of six rifle companies reached the far riverbank. Eventually, only a few dozen survivors of these companies of the 141st Infantry

Regiment made it back to their lines on the eastern side of the Rapido. Clark now ordered Keyes to resume the attack with the surviving battalions of the 143rd Infantry Regiment. At 1600hrs on 21 January, under a heavy artillery screen, the 143rd Infantry Regiment made a second river crossing attempt. Only a total of five infantry companies were to comprise the American bridgehead on the western side of the Rapido. However, before dawn on 22 January, this salient had been eliminated by a Nazi counter-attack. The Fifth Army's initial assault on the Gustav Line and access to the Liri Valley south of Cassino, after initial optimism at Clark's headquarters, was halted by 22 January.

With the successful British crossing of the Garigliano River, the movement of the Hermann Göring Panzer Division to France was delayed and the battered remnants of the 90th Panzer Grenadier Division were deployed from the Adriatic Front to the Aurunci mountain range. Vietinghoff also brought the 29th Panzer Grenadier Division south from Rome to reinforce his line holding Cassino to the north and the Rapido River defences to the south.

The failed crossing of the Rapido River on 20 – 22 January 1944 changed the axes of the FEC and US 34th divisions' advance. The two FEC divisions continued their attack north of Cassino towards Atina across the Rapido River, where the river turns and runs to the north-east. The 2nd Moroccan Division breached the Gustav Line on 24 January and captured Monte Santa Croce. The 3rd Algerian Division crossed the Rapido in the vicinity of Sant' Elia Flumerapido and moved westward to parallel the US 34th Division's prior river assault, also to the north of Cassino opposite an enemy sector extending from Monte Cassino to Caira. The 34th Division's objective was to force its way into the Gustav Line south of Caira, then turn southwards to attack Monte Cassino from the north and also seize the distant heights beyond it topped by Monte Cairo.

After confronting enemy minefields and flooded terrain over the next few days, a very tenuous bridgehead on the western bank was established by elements of the 133rd Infantry Regiment, which Ryder tried to reinforce, but a withdrawal back across the river ensued. The US 135th Infantry Regiment's attack, likewise to the north of the town of Cassino, amounted to no gains. The 34th's 168th Infantry Regiment crossed the river further to the north opposite Caira on 27 January but the advance was stalled by Nazi counter-attacks, despite some limited American tank support. Two days later, after more American tanks arrived, the 133rd Infantry Regiment resumed its advance while elements of the 135th Infantry Regiment reached the environs of the town of Cassino. On 30 January, the 168th Infantry Regiment did successfully cross the Rapido River and took Caira and the surrounding heights.

Juin's 3rd Algerian Division, operating to the north of the US 34th Division, captured Colle Belvedere across the road to Atina, on 26 January and moved on Monte Abate the next day. However, the FEC forces were counter-attacked by elements of

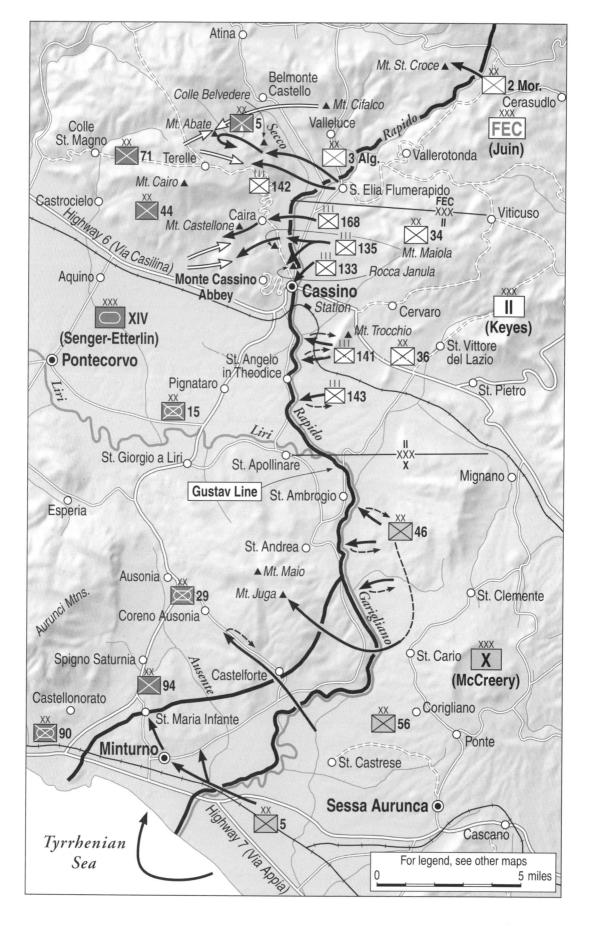

Atina

Mt. St. Croce ▲

XX
2 Mor.

Cerasudlo

Belmonte
Castello

Colle Belvedere

Mt. Cifalco ▲

Valleluce

XXX
FEC
(Juin)

Vallerotonda

Mt. Abate

XX
5

Secco

XX
3 Alg.

Colle
St. Magno

XX
71

Terelle

Castrocielo

Mt. Cairo ▲

XX
142

S. Elia Flumerapido

XX
44

Caira

Mt. Castellone ▲

III
168

FEC
XXX
II

Viticuso

XX
34

Mt. Maiola

Highway 6 (Via Casilina)

III
135

III
133

Rocca Janula

Monte Cassino Abbey

Cassino

Station

Cervaro

II
(Keyes)

XXX

Aquino

XXX
XIV
(Senger-Etterlin)

Pontecorvo

Mt. Trocchio ▲

III
141

St. Vittore
del Lazio

XX
36

St. Pietro

St. Angelo
in Theodice

III
143

Pignataro

XX
15

St. Giorgio a Liri

Liri

Rapido

II
XXX
X

Mignano

St. Apollinare

Gustav Line

St. Ambrogio

Esperia

XX
46

St. Andrea

Mt. Maio ▲

St. Clemente

Ausonia

XX
29

Mt. Juga ▲

Garigliano

Coreno Ausonia

Aurunci Mtns.

St. Cario

XXX
X
(McCreery)

Spigno Saturnia

Ausente

Castelforte

XX
94

Castellonorato

St. Maria Infante

Corigliano

XX
90

XX
56

Minturno

Ponte

St. Castrese

Sessa Aurunca

Tyrrhenian
Sea

Highway 7 (Via Appia)

XX
5

Cascano

For legend, see other maps

0   5 miles

the German 44th Infantry Division, which managed to evict the Tunisian 4th Rifle Regiment from Monte Abate, and maintain possession of it from Juin's attempts to re-take the height. Keyes reinforced the 3rd Algerian Division with the US 36th Division's 142nd Infantry Regiment, which had not participated in the Rapido crossing debacle days before, to advance southward on Monte Cassino from the Colle Belvedere area. The Americans and North Africans were approaching Monte Cassino with higher enemy-controlled positions, such as Montes Cairo and Abate, to the north-west that were able to direct artillery fire on the Allied advance.

Slow progress was made by the Allies amid the northern outskirts of Cassino during the first few days of February 1944. Despite heavy casualties, the 135th Infantry Regiment seized the commanding height of Monte Castellone on 1 February. On 5 February, elements of the 135th Infantry Regiment were as close as 1,000 yards from the walls of the Benedictine abbey atop Monte Cassino. The US 168th Infantry Regiment came to within several hundred yards of Mount Calvary, a tactical key point overlooking Monte Cassino, which was to change hands among the combatants during the initial ten days of February. During the night of 5–6 February, the 168th directly assaulted Monte Cassino via a deep gorge, but had to withdraw from heavy German fire above them.

Then the Germans, replete with fresh *panzergrenadier* and paratroop reinforcements, launched their counter-attack and drove the Americans back. The remaining battalions of the 34th Division were ineffective in a renewed assault on 11 February to seize Monastery Hill and the town of Cassino, as Nazi artillery and mortars stopped them within a few hundred yards of their rocky positions. If they had been successful, the 4th Indian and 2nd New Zealand divisions were prepared to move through them and exploit the breakthrough. However, only evacuation of the dead and wounded American troops occurred with the New Zealand and Indian troops taking over their positions. The First Battle of Cassino had ended with the Germans in possession of the town, the monastery and the surrounding heights to the north-west of Monte Cassino.

Fifth Army crossings of the Garigliano and Rapido rivers and the First Battle of Cassino, January 1944. The Fifth Army's British X Corps (under McCreery) 5th, 46th and 56th divisions, the US II Corps (under Keyes) 34th and 36th divisions, and the French Expeditionary Corps (FEC, under Juin) 2nd Moroccan and 3rd Algerian divisions attacks on the Gustav Line from 17–24 January 1944 are shown. These savage Garigliano and Rapido river assaults culminated in the First Battle of Cassino, which lasted until the end of the first week of February 1944. By this time, the Fifth Army formations had utterly exhausted themselves combating the German XIV Corps (under Senger und Etterlin), initially composed of the 44th, 71st and 94th Infantry, the 15th, 29th and 90th Panzergrenadier, and 5th Mountain divisions. These tenacious Nazi units held the Gustav Line from the Tyrrhenian Sea in the west to the heights of the Apennine Mountains in the middle of the Italian Peninsula. Major elements of Heidrich's German 1st Parachute Division were also deployed in the Cassino sector and played a pivotal defensive role in the First Battle of Cassino. (*Philip Schwartzberg, Meridian Mapping, Minneapolis, MN*)

(**Above**) On 20 September, an Eighth Army reconnaissance unit, seated atop its armoured car, met US paratroopers of the 82nd Airborne Division at Auletta, 20 miles east of Eboli. Also on that day, Montgomery's troops reached Potenza, 50 miles east of Salerno, and severed the east-west highway from Bari on the Adriatic Sea to the Tyrrhenian coast battlefield. The arrival of the Eighth Army's vanguard had no influence on the outcome of the Salerno battle, as the Fifth Army had fought it out alone against the German Tenth Army. (*NARA*)

(**Opposite**) A heavily laden British M4 medium tank of the 7th Armoured Division moving through the streets of Cava, 6 miles to the north-west of the town of Salerno, with two British infantrymen (*foreground*). Cava was located in the vicinity of the important Molina Pass in the mountains north of the fishing village of Vietri, which had been assaulted and defended by the 2nd Special Service Brigade of Commandos during the Salerno battles. (*NARA*)

(**Opposite, above**) Infantrymen of the US 3rd Division entering Avellino several days after the Salerno battle had been won. Avellino, located 30 miles to the east of Naples on the Sabato River and on the Foggia-Naples road, was the site where American paratroopers of the 2nd Battalion, 509th Parachute Infantry Regiment (PIR), staged a diversionary drop on the night of 14 September 1943, while the beachhead battles at Salerno raged. The VI Corps, now comprising the US 45th and 3rd Infantry divisions, was tasked to seize the Avellino-Montemaraano–Teora line, while maintaining close contact with the Eighth Army's left flank. (*NARA*)

(**Above**) American soldiers entering Acerno, 9 miles north-east of Naples, as they passed a disabled Nazi Flak 88 anti-aircraft (AA) anti-tank (AT) gun on 22 September 1943. Demolished bridges and German rearguards had delayed the advance of the 3rd Infantry Division from the south. The division's leading regiment had to conduct cross-country marches through the mountains to outflank the German positions to seize the town. (*NARA*)

(**Opposite, below**) American troops from the US 82nd Airborne Division and Darby's Rangers aboard their truck passing through the rubble of a civilian-lined street in Naples on 1 October 1943. Neapolitan partisans had fought to keep their city from being totally destroyed by the retreating Germans. (*NARA*)

British X Corps infantrymen marching in single file along a muddy track paralleling a railway line during the advance towards the Volturno River, north of Naples, in early October 1943. At this time, the term 'Sunny Italy' was no longer applicable as torrential rains started to swell rivers and turn dirt roads into deep muddy tracks. Mud became a major factor in delaying the Fifth Army's advance until mid-October. The Allies were to reach the fortified Volturno River by the end of the first week of October. After arriving along the southern bank of the river, X Corps, the Fifth Army's left flank, met strong resistance from the 15th Panzer Grenadier and Hermann Göring divisions between Capua and the Tyrrhenian coast. (*NARA*)

(**Opposite, above**) Soldiers of the US Fifth Army marching across a treadway supported by pontoons across the swollen Volturno River, 35 miles north of Naples. The initial advance for the Allies to capture Rome was slowed by the German defence of this natural barrier. After gaining a foothold along the northern bank of the Volturno River, Clark's Fifth Army was to face other obstacles, including the hastily erected temporary defences of the Barbara Line, which ran from the Tyrrhenian Sea through Teano into the Matese Mountains south of Venafro and Isernia. (*NARA*)

(**Opposite, below**) An X Corps British ambulance crossing the Volturno River over a steel treadway bridge supported by pontoons. During the Volturno's crossing in mid-October 1943, the US 45th Division turned the XIV Panzer Corps' left flank in the vicinity of the Calore River's convergence with the Volturno near Amorosi, to the east of Caiazzo. The Germans were compelled to withdraw on 16 October and the entire river was in the Fifth Army's possession three days later. (*NARA*)

(**Opposite, above**) Infantrymen of the British 56th Division passing German road signs as they entered Capua, south of the Volturno River, 15 miles north of Naples on Highway 6. This town had been under heavy Nazi artillery shelling from the northern bank of the river. The Fifth Army's next move entailed the US VI Corps to advance along Highway 6 and the valley north of the winding Volturno River. McCreery's British X Corps was to move north of the Castel Volturno–Grazzanise–Capua Line, with the 46th Division on the left, the 7th Armoured Division in the centre and the 56th Division on the right, towards the Italian mountain chain south of the Garigliano River, which were all situated behind the temporary fortifications of the Barbara Line running from Mondragone on the Tyrrhenian coast through Teano, the latter located just to the west of Highway 6 to the north-west of Capua. (*NARA*)

(**Opposite, below**) A Canadian artillery observation post is situated in its slit trench near Potenza, which was located above the Basento River halfway between Taranto, 50 miles to the south-east, and Salerno. This important road and railway centre in the foothills of the Apennine Mountains, which connected to the port of Bari on the Adriatic Sea, had been subjected to a six-day Allied aerial bombardment that commenced on 13 September 1943. This medieval Italian town was ultimately seized by an infantry brigade, reinforced with some armour and artillery, from the 1st Canadian Division on 20 September 1943. (*NARA*)

(**Above**) A battery of Canadian 25-pounder field artillery pieces firing on Potenza. Most of the route for the Canadian reinforced brigade towards Potenza was over narrow mountain roads. In addition, the Canadians had to contend with firefights from the rearguards of retreating German columns and demolished bridges over tributaries to the Basento River. Potenza's major tactical advantage for the enemy was its commanding position above the wide river flats. This offered the Nazi infantry, a company of the German 3rd Parachute Regiment, 1st Parachute Division, supported by machine-guns, an excellent field of fire in defence of the town to delay the Canadian advance. By 1930hrs on 19 September 1943, the lead vehicles of motorised Canadian infantry, the West Albertas, were on the high ground overlooking the Basento valley with the town of Potenza spread out over the hillside. (*NARA*)

(**Above**) A Universal carrier with a mounted Vickers medium machine-gun from a platoon of the Saskatoon Light Infantry support battalion firing in direct support of the attack on Potenza on 20 September. An *ad hoc* brigade-sized formation, built around the infantry elements from the West Nova Scotia, the Carleton and York, and the Royal 22nd Regiments of the 1st Canadian Division, was assembled for the assault. By midday, after a delay from German landmines and demolitions, which had kept the Canadian armour at bay, tanks of the 14th Calgary Armoured Regiment cleared the remaining obstacles on the main road and entered the town. With Potenza's capture, the Eighth and Fifth armies linked up at Auletta, 20 miles to the west, establishing a continuous Allied line from Bari on the Adriatic coast to Salerno. (*NARA*)

(**Opposite, above**) An Eighth Army infantryman cautiously moving around a street in Termoli in early October 1943. Two brigades from the British 78th Division, reinforced with Commandos, amphibiously landed north of the mouth of the Biferno River at Termoli on 3 October. The 78th Division's 11th Brigade fought its way across the Biferno south of the town. Nazi forces that defended Termoli from this Eighth Army move included elements of the *Luftwaffe's* 1st Parachute, the 29th Panzergrenadier and 26th Panzer divisions. The German 16th Panzer Division was also dispatched by Kesselring from the Fifth Army Front to deal with this threat. Both British and Canadian armour played a pivotal role as three days of fighting ensued against the German units, which were forced to withdraw to the north of the Trigno River after the port town was finally secured by the Allies on 7 October. (*NARA*)

(**Opposite, below**) A German soldier's grave is marked by his coal scuttle-shaped helmet next to a wrecked German Mk IV Panzer of the 16th Panzer Division after the fighting at Termoli concluded at the end of the first week of October 1943. The Eighth Army's advance to Termoli comprised two divisions: the British 78th Division on the Adriatic coast's Highway 16; and the 1st Canadian Division, which trekked through the mountains along Highway 17. Two days after the initial British entry into Termoli on 3 October, German tanks and infantry counter-attacked, but were stopped by British and Canadian armour, the latter from the Three Rivers Regiment. (*NARA*)

An infantryman from the 3rd Infantry Brigade, 1st Canadian Division in XIII Corps was felled by a German sniper's bullet in Campochiaro on 23 October 1943. Campochiaro was situated 12 miles to the south-west of Campobasso in the vicinity of Vinchiaturo on Highway 17 in central Italy. During the autumn, the Canadians faced inclement rainy weather in addition to the difficult inland high ground on the north-eastward axis of Highway 17 heading towards Termoli on the Adriatic coast. The Germans had made the best tactical use of the terrain and conducted tenacious stands in each mountain village. At Motta, the Germans held off the advancing Canadians for a full day. It took the Canadians three days to secure Vinchiaturo between Cantalupo to the north-west and Campobasso to the north-east on Highway 17. (*NARA*)

An Eighth Army motorised column negotiating muddy tracks along the Trigno River at the end of October 1943. The Trigno River was wide and situated below high banks with the Germans positioned along the north bank. On the night of 27–28 October, several battalions of the 78th Division attempted to force a crossing. The attackers met with heavy mortar, artillery and machine-gunfire from the German defenders, and it was not until 3 November that British tanks of the 46th Royal Tank Regiment made it across the Trigno with the assistance of bulldozers and sappers to negotiate the river's high banks. (NARA)

(**Above**) A Vickers medium machine-gun crew in their camouflaged position along the Sangro River Front in late November 1943. Some of the snow-capped mountains, situated between the Trigno and Sangro rivers, through which V Corps trekked east of the Apennines, are shown. Once situated, this machine-gun was crewed by two soldiers. One fired the weapons while a second man held and fed the ammunition belt. The maximal operational range of the Vickers medium machine-gun was over 4,000 yards, making it superb for indirect fire support. (*NARA*)

(**Opposite, above**) A Universal carrier of a an anti-tank (AT) unit of a Sikh regiment in the 8th Indian Division of V Corps towing a 6-pounder AT gun over mesh-matting up the far bank of the Sangro River in late November 1943. The Indians had to contend with a very tenacious defence from elements of four German divisions: the 16th and 26th Panzer, the 29th Panzergrenadier and the 1st Parachute. At the fortified village of Mozzogrogna, to the north of the Sangro River, the Indians were held up by the enemy counter-attacking with tanks and flame-throwers. (*NARA*)

(**Opposite, below**) A Bren-gun team of the Loyal Edmonton Regiment of the 2nd Canadian Infantry Brigade, 1st Canadian Division, taking up a supportive firing position in the coastal city of Ortona at the end of December 1943. The approach to Ortona had also been difficult for the Canadians as they had to cross the Moro River and nearby ridges, all defended by elements of the German 90th Panzer Grenadier, 26th Panzer and 1st Parachute divisions. The Eighth Army advance into Ortona was led by this regiment along with the Seaforth Highlanders of Canada. (*NARA*)

Canadian infantrymen readying their Mills bombs amid the rubble of the former Bank of Naples in Ortona for a raid on a German machine-gun position. German demolition teams had been expert at creating excellent firing positions for machine-gunners, snipers, *panzerfaust* teams, and had also booby trapped the ruins of the town's buildings, which took its toll on both Canadian infantry and armour. (*NARA*)

(**Opposite, above**) A 6-pounder anti-tank (AT) gun of the 1st Regiment Royal Canadian Horse Artillery, after being manually wheeled into position, firing on a German 1st Parachute Division redoubt amid Ortona's rubble at the edge of the town on 21 December. Heavy fighting, usually house-to-house, went on for a full week on this Adriatic coast town. After the capture of Ortona, the Canadians became experts at urban fighting against the determined German foe in Europe. (*NARA*)

(**Opposite, below**) Many of the elements involved in the horrific combat at Ortona during the week of 21–28 December are displayed above. They include a Canadian M4 medium tank, a German Pak 40 75mm anti-tank (AT) gun, aggressive Canadian infantry and an Italian town's rubble, in large part created by German sappers for defence purposes. Often Canadian tanks, after climbing over piles of rocks and debris, exposed their vulnerable bellies to German AT gunfire and *panzerfaust* projectiles. The Pak 75mm AT gun was introduced in early 1942, and was quite effective at penetrating most enemy armour, although the weapon's excessive weight limited its mobility. However, in fixed positions, as at Ortona, many Canadian Sherman tanks were destroyed. On 28 December, elements of the Princess Patricia's Canadian Light Infantry (PPCLI) made contact with another battle-hardened unit, the 48th Highlanders of Canada, which had struggled in their northward combat trek to the west of Ortona. (*NARA*)

(**Above**) British infantrymen of the 1st London Scottish Regiment of the 56th Division climbing over a stone wall while on patrol on Monte Camino's Monastery Hill in early December 1943. The Mignano Gap, which had to be cleared to get to Monte Cassino and the Liri Valley, was enclosed by the heavily defended Nazi positions atop Montes Camino, la Difensa, and Lungo on the left-hand side of the valley, and Montes Sammucro and Rotondo on the right. The British 56th Division was assigned the initial assault of Monte Camino on 5 November. Monte Camino has been described as 'a mountain of steep and rocky slopes and razorback spurs with very little cover', and it had a monastery at its peak. While the British were able to seize Calabritto at the base of Monte Camino, the height remained in the hands of the German 15th Panzer Grenadier Division, which had meticulously mined and booby trapped the approaches to the summit. After five days halfway up Monte Camino, the 56th Division's leading two were exhausted and only had limited supplies to defend against the Nazi counter-attacks, necessitating a withdrawal during the night of 14 November. The fighting for Monte Camino was renewed by X Corps on 1 December, but it would not be until 10 December before this 963m height was seized and cleared of the German defenders. (*USAMHI*)

(**Opposite, above**) Infantrymen of the French Expeditionary Corps (FEC) of the Fifth Army, are shown warily passing a destroyed German Panzer III tank north of the town of Cassino in January 1944. The two major FEC formations, the 2nd Moroccan and 3rd Algerian divisions, both successfully crossed the Rapido River north of Cassino during the last week of January to coincide with the II Corps' 34th and 35th divisions' attacks. (*NARA*)

(**Opposite, below**) A trio from the Canadian–American elite 1st Special Service Force taking cover in a pile of rocks and firing at German positions while on patrol in Monte Maio in early January 1944. This objective had come on the heels of their previous feat of capturing Monte la Difensa, an extremely difficult height in the Montes Camino/ la Difensa/Maggiore hill mass. This force proved instrumental at breaking the stalemate in seizing the requisite defended heights in order to approach Cassino and the Liri Valley through the Mignano Gap. (*NARA*)

(**Opposite, above**) British infantrymen patrolling a hillside in the Garigliano River sector of McCreery's X Corps. On 4 January 1944, X Corps made an unsuccessful attempt to seize Cedro Hill, a height of 500, feet under direct German observation from Monte Porchia. On 17 January, the British 5th, 46th and 56th divisions launched their more successful attacks across the Garigliano River at separate points along the waterway's length. (*USAMHI*)

(**Above**) A British infantry Vickers medium machine-gun support squad marching along the X Corps Garigliano River sector in early January 1944. While advancing, a Vickers machine-gun squad comprising six men: two to service the weapon when in action, while the other four carried extra barrels, ammunitions boxes, and personal weapons. (*NARA*)

(**Opposite, below**) British gunners checking ammunition and setting the fuses for their 5.5-inch calibre artillery piece, situated on the Garigliano River Front just prior to the X Corps attacks in mid-January 1944. This gun had a range of 16,000 yards with a 100lb shell and 18,600 with an 80lb shell. The X Corps crossed the Garigliano River on 17 January, despite the enormous number of mines planted by the Germans on the waterway's banks. As ten British battalions crossed the river and established a bridgehead by the next day, Kesselring shifted the 90th and 29th Panzer Grenadier divisions from the north near Rome to augment the German 94th Infantry Division's ability to contest the crossing, thereby limiting the extent to which McCreery's objectives were seized, especially in light of the failed British 46th Division crossing to the south of the US II attacks across the Rapido River. (*NARA*)

(**Opposite, above**) British X Corps soldiers, in leather jerkins, ferrying captured German troops back across the Garigliano River to Allied lines on 21 January 1944. The X Corps crossings of the Garigliano River were made, in large part, with paddled wooden assault boats, as flooding of the waterway prevented the installation of adequate Bailey or treadway bridging. German prisoners reported that Nazi defenders were placing extensive supply installations and defensive positions around Cassino. Allied intelligence rated the German positions behind the Garigliano and Rapido rivers as some of the strongest defensive zones south of Rome. (*NARA*)

(**Opposite, below**) Volunteers from the Canadian-American 1st Special Service Force (SSF) preparing to be the first across the Rapido River in their light T24 carrier. The US II Corps was ordered to cross the river to facilitate a main attack along Highway 6 west of Monte Cassino. The US 36th Division's 141st and 143rd regiments, veterans of the Salerno landings, were to lead the assault across the Rapido River. After penetrating the Gustav Line, the US 1st Armoured Division was to pass through the infantry and move through the Liri Valley to Rome. The Americans were met and repulsed by the German 15th Panzer Grenadier Division, with the 3rd Panzer Grenadier Division at Arce located nearby in the middle of the Liri Valley. (*USAMHI*)

(**Above**) American infantrymen experimenting with smoke pots that were to be used to aid in obscuring the crossing of the Rapido River, which two regiments of the US 36th Division assaulted abreast of one another on the evening of 20 January 1944. Many of the 141st Infantry Regiment's assault boats were destroyed by enemy gunfire even before reaching the river's edge. The wooden craft were necessary because the river's swift current and German artillery fire had precluded the construction of bridges. (*USAMHI*)

(**Above**) US 36th Division infantrymen marching towards the Rapido River with smoke pots to mask the approach from Nazi gunners. Only 100 troops of the 141st Infantry Regiment made it across and then could not be reinforced. The 143rd Infantry Regiment did have a few of its companies make it to the far bank, but then German gunfire compelled the regimental commander to withdraw his men back to the river's eastern bank. (*USAMHI*)

(**Opposite, above**) An 81mm mortar crew of the 141st Infantry Regiment, US 36th Division, firing rounds in advance of its infantrymen's attempted crossing of the Rapido River on 20–21 January 1944. The M1 mortar was capable of sending a high-explosive (HE) shell, which had fins for flight stabilisation since the barrel was smooth-bore, almost 3,300 yards. Also, smoke and flare shells were able to be lobbed by this infantry support weapon. After its initial repulse on 20 January, the 141st again assaulted across the Rapido River. Effective Nazi artillery and mortar fire destroyed bridges and boats and only a few score of men from these attacking companies made it back to their lines, with the rest of their force either killed or captured. (*USAMHI*)

(**Opposite, below**) American medics and soldiers from the US 36th Division bringing back dead and wounded from the Rapido River crossings of 20–21 January 1944. After the ill-fated crossing attempts, the waterway received the dubious moniker 'Bloody River'. (*NARA*)

An American 57mm M1 anti-tank (AT) gun-crew preparing its heavily camouflaged weapon for a Nazi counter-attack in the Rapido River sector after the failed 20 – 21 January 1944 crossings by the 141st and 143rd Infantry regiments of the US 36th Division. This gun was a towed weapon that was based on the British 6-pounder AT gun. In February 1941, US Army Ordnance started adapting the 6-pounder for American production to supply the British through Lend-Lease. (NARA)

Epilogue

The cost in combatant and civilian life during the invasion of the Italian mainland from early September 1943 to the stalemate on the Gustav Line in early February 1944 was horrific. During Salerno's Operation Avalanche, the Nazis inflicted approximately 2,000 killed, 7,000 wounded and 3,500 missing, while they incurred 3,500 casualties, of whom 600 were killed.

Other locales were similarly bloody. The British bore the brunt of the casualties with over 600 men lost at the Volturno River crossing. At Monte Camino, the British 46th and 56th divisions of X Corps suffered 1,000 casualties to conquer this height. At San Pietro, over 1,500 total US casualties were incurred in a ten-day battle. Since crossing the Sangro River, the New Zealand Division alone had suffered over 1,600 casualties. From 20–28 December, almost 500 German paratroop casualties were incurred before and during the seizure of Ortona on the Adriatic coast. The 36th Division, which had weathered the Nazi beach defences and counter-attacks at Salerno, had reaped a terrible toll in casualties in their two-day Rapido River assault, with over 140 dead, roughly 700 wounded and almost 900 missing. The excessive butcher's bill had even generated a post-war Congressional inquiry into the circumstances and outcome of the deadly attack by the Texas Division's 141st and 143rd infantry regiments. After the First Battle of Cassino concluded in early February 1944, only 25 per cent of the combined 3,200-man initial strength of the US 34th Division's 135th and 168th infantry regiments remained from the offensive north of Cassino that had started on 24 January with their Rapido River crossings.

Italian citizens paid a steep price for the Allied endeavour to liberate their country from the Nazi yoke. This was exemplified at Potenza, where over 2,000 civilian casualties with over 200 dead were incurred, mostly from the previous Allied aerial bombardment of that centrally located Italian mountain town. Many more Italians were to succumb as non-combatant casualties from the ubiquitous scourges of armed conflict: famine, disease, exposure, pestilence, reprisals and harsh treatment by warring forces.

A Royal Army Medical Corps (RAMC) contingent attending a wounded X Corps soldier at a dressing station on the Garigliano River Front in mid-January 1944. The medical corpsman in the centre is holding a bottle of plasma to replace some of the lost blood volume from his wounds. The German defensive works behind the Garigliano River were formidable, as the Nazis blasted gun pits out of the natural rocky terrain and created clear fields of fire for their camouflaged rifle pits, concrete-reinforced bunkers and steel-turreted machine-gun emplacements, all covered by minefields and wire entanglements. (NARA)

Canadian casualties are loaded into an ambulance by members of the Royal Canadian Army Medical Corps (RCAMC) for evacuation to a rear-echelon regimental aid post (RAP), usually located near the forward regimental headquarters in the Moro River area just to the south of Ortona on the Adriatic coast, in December 1943. The Moro River Canadian Cemetery has almost 1,400 graves of soldiers who perished in this sector of the Eighth Army. Many from the Princess Patricia's Canadian Light Infantry of the 2nd Canadian Infantry Brigade (CIB) died during their night assault on Villa Rogatti near the Moro. Shrapnel from mortar rounds, machine-gunfire, as well as hand-to-hand combat wounds were encountered during the Canadians' battle there. (NARA)

A temporary British battlefield cemetery, marked by crosses, steel helmets and the venerable Short Magazine Lee-Enfield (SMLE) rifles, for three X Corps soldiers is serenely situated atop the Damano Summit on the Garigliano River Front near the town of Castelforte in the British 56th Division sector in January 1944. Two brigades from this British infantry formation had crossed the Garigliano in wooden assault boats in the vicinity of Castelforte on 17 January after a concentrated artillery barrage by X Corps guns. The British did establish a small lodgement on the far bank at considerable cost from enemy artillery and mortar fire. (*NARA*)

(**Opposite, above**) A British burial detail is doing its grim work in a field along the coastal plain of Salerno. During the massive German counter-attacks of 12–14 September 1943, the British 56th Division was in the open plain south-east of Battipaglia, with its positions in full view of German artillery spotters, which directed enemy shellfire on the X Corps troops. On 13 September, while German artillery shelled the British 46th Division dug into the hills about the town of Salerno, German Panzers attacked the 56th Division's lines from Battipaglia. Elements of the Coldstream Guards and 9th Battalion, Royal Fusiliers stubbornly held their ground for several hours, with many making the ultimate sacrifice. (*NARA*)

(**Opposite, below**) An American medical team from the 4th Naval Battalion going through the effects of a US 36th Division infantryman killed beside his Jeep on one of the landing beaches south of the Sele River near Paestum on D-Day for Operation Avalanche, 9 September 1943. The 141st and 142nd regimental combat teams (RCTs) of the 'Texas' Division made the assault in six waves at eight-minute intervals onto the Paestum beaches without a preparatory naval or air bombardment. The 142nd RCT was pinned down by German machine-gunners of the 16th Panzer Division in the 50-foot Tower of Paestum. Other assault troops were fired upon by Nazi positions sheltered by the dunes overlooking the landing beaches. The combat during the initial assault was intense, with many American infantrymen killed or wounded by enemy machine-gunfire as only scrub growth and shallow irrigation ditches provided cover on the assault beaches. (*NARA*)

(**Opposite, above**) The graves of five Canadian gunners on a ridgeline overlooking the Adriatic coastal village of San Vito, on the approaches to the Moro River to the south of Ortona in January 1944. The surrounding countryside was dotted with stone farmhouses amid olive orchards and vineyards. It was on 8 December 1943, in this idyllic setting, that the artillery regiments of the 1st Canadian Division opened up with a tremendous barrage on enemy positions along the northern ridgeline of the Moro valley. In proximity to San Vito, Canadian 25-pounder batteries, in deeply mudded positions, hurled over a thousand shells every minute at the Germans. (*NARA*)

(**Opposite, below**) A dead German paratrooper in his smock lying amid photographs of Hitler and other German military on the outskirts of Ortona. Most battalions of the German 1st Parachute Division started entering the defensive line at Ortona on 20 December 1943, much to the relief of the decimated 90th Panzer Grenadier Division. Paratroop after-action reports touted that their defensive tactics were well-employed, with few costly counter-attacks on the advancing Canadians. Unlike the *panzergrenadiers*, the German parachutists seldom surrendered *en masse* at Ortona with over a hundred corpses found by the Canadians in the town for mass burial. (*NARA*)

(**Above**) Two British soldiers kneeling to examine the graves of two German soldiers that were near Caserta during the autumn of 1943. On 2 October, elements of the British 56th and 7th Armoured divisions headed north-west from Naples and, against decreasing Nazi resistance, marched through Caserta in their trek to the southern bank of the Volturno River in the Capua area. Five days later, X Corps would be on the river in strength. During the previous century, both Caserta and Capua had been prominent combat sites for Garibaldi's troops fighting Bourbon troops during the Italian Unification battles of 1860. Such was the geographic crossroads location of Italy, Sicily and Malta, among other MTO locales that had brought centuries of conflict to these lands and peoples. Mussolini's ouster followed by the Italian capitulation, produced havoc and hardship for Italy as the Germans chose to contest the entire length of the peninsula, beginning at Salerno and continuing through the stalemated First Battle of Cassino at the Nazi Gustav Line. (*NARA*)

References

Atkinson, R. (2007), *The Day of Battle: The War in Sicily and Italy, 1943–1944*, Holt Paperbacks, New York.

Black, R.W. (1992), *Rangers in World War II*, Ivy Books, New York.

Blumenson, M. (2001), *Anzio: The Gamble that Failed*, Cooper Square Press, New York.

Blumenson, M. (1970), *The Mediterranean Theater of Operations: Salerno to Cassino*, US Government Printing Office, Washington, DC.

Carver, M. (2002), *The Imperial War Museum Book of the War in Italy 1943–1945*, Pan Books, London.

D'Este, C. (1991), *Fatal Decision: Anzio and the Battle for Rome*, Harper Collins, New York.

D'Este, C. (1990), *World War II in the Mediterranean 1942–1945*, Algonquin Books, Chapel Hill.

Diamond, J. (2017), *First Blood in North Africa: Operation Torch and the US Campaign in Africa in World War II*, Stackpole Books, Guilford.

Diamond, J. (2017), *The Invasion of Sicily 1943*, Pen & Sword, Barnsley.

Ellis, J. (1984), *Cassino: The Hollow Victory*, Aurum Press.

Ford, K. (2004), *Cassino 1944: Breaking the Gustav Line*, Osprey Publishing. Oxford.

Graham, D. (1970), *Cassino*, Ballentine, New York.

Konstam, A. (2013), *Salerno 1943: The Allies Invade Southern Italy*, Osprey Publishing, Oxford.

Mason, D. (1972), *Salerno: Foothold in Europe*, Ballentine, New York.

Neillands, R. (2004), *Eighth Army: The Triumphant Desert Army that Held the Axis at Bay from North Africa to the Alps, 1939–45*, Overlook Press, Woodstock.

Perret, G. (1991), *There's a War to be Won: The United States Army in World War II*, Ballentine Books, New York.

Porch, D. (2004), *The Path to Victory: The Mediterranean Theater in World War II*, Farrar, Straus and Giroux, New York.

Tucker-Jones, A. (2013), *Armoured Warfare in the Italian Campaign 1943–1945*, Pen & Sword, Barnsley.

Werner, B. (2015), *Storming Monte La Difensa: The First Special Service Force at the Winter Line, Italy 1943*, Osprey Publishing, Oxford.

Whitlock, F. (1999), *The Rock of Anzio. From Sicily to Dachau: A History of the US 45th Infantry Division*, Westview Press, Boulder.

Zuehlke, M. (2003), *Ortona: Canada's Epic World War II Battle*, Douglas & McIntyre, Madeira Park.